On The Deer Path

On The Deer Path

David Baylr Be
Feb 2013

DAVID BARRINGTON BARNES

Published in 2012 by David Barrington Barnes

A catalogue record for this book is available from the British Library

ISBN 978-0-9572893-0-7

The website for this book is www.onthedeerpath.co.uk

Printed and Bound in Great Britain by
CPI Antony Rowe, Chippenham and Eastbourne

TO VIRGINIA

"Better to hunt in fields for health unbought,
Than fee the doctor for a nauseous draft.
The wise for cure on exercise depend;
God never made his work, for man to mend."

John Dryden 1700.

Contents

Introduction

I am a lucky man: I have a passion for field sports. In particular, I love deerstalking. This memoir is my best shot at sharing my enjoyment of it with others.

It is not intended to instruct anybody in the art of low ground stalking. There are already a number of books on the subject, written by skilled exponents. There are also many training courses provided by deer and shooting organisations. As I am a clumsy stalker, an indifferent shot and an amateur naturalist I have no expertise to offer and am not trying to match any of these. Nor have I written this book for the elucidation of folk who are ignorant of deerstalking or, for whatever reason, against it, although some of these might benefit from reading it.

This book celebrates my enthusiasm for low ground stalking. I have changed the names of some persons and places in it for the protection of their privacy. Otherwise, the anecdotes and incidents in it are all true and are culled from very many more which I think are as interesting, but which I do not have space to retail here. I hope other deerstalkers and hunters generally will enjoy these and, perhaps recognise the tales I have told. If, through it's pages, I succeed in informing or persuading just a few persons of the pleasure to be had whilst out in the country-side, in pursuit of deer, then this memoir will have fulfilled its purpose.

In the years since I became a deerstalker, I have spent many hours in and about my mainly solitary pursuit. Insofar as I have shared my stalking with other deerstalkers, and there have been several of them, I thank them for their enthusiasm and congeniality. Now I stretch out a hand to my readers and invite them to be my companions in my various outings down the paths of the deer.

Acknowledgements

I am obliged to the Duke of Sutherland for writing the Foreword.

I wish to thank my wife, Virginia, for proof reading the manuscript. Theresa Gibbs has with great patience organised this as a Word document. Geoff Fisher has converted this draft and produced a book whilst providing friendly expertise. John Thornley, O.B.E, has given me help and encouragement.

Roe Stalking" by Mick Cawston is reproduced with kind permission by Sally Mitchell Fine Arts Ltd. on the cover of this book.

My photograph was taken by the German sportsman, Magnus Eger

The well known wildlife artist, Hans Bulder (www.hansbulder.com) has generously permitted me to reproduce his evocative drawing of a roe buck head in each chapter heading. Peter Carr, the Editor of SPORTING RIFLE has also encouraged me, as have other deerstalkers.

I thank all these persons for their assistance but any errors or defects are mine.

Foreword

I was delighted to be asked to write a brief foreword by David Barrington Barnes to his low ground deerstalking memories.

On the Cambridgeshire/Suffolk borders we have the usual complement of deer species from fallow down to muntjac, and we did have quite a herd of red deer until someone else decided to cull them – they are now extinct as far as we are concerned. It was after this incident that I got to know David. His instincts accord with mine in that we try to manage the deer by selective shooting to achieve the balance of ages and sexes. The taking of animals for the sake of trophy heads does not come into the thinking.

To this end David has been managing our deer and those of some of our neighbours for many years. The success of his stewardship can be seen in the health of the deer, while controlling numbers to limit the damage to crops and trees.

I always wondered how David managed his legal practice as well as our deer, I assumed one side of many consultations was conducted by mobile telephone from a high seat half way up an old oak tree with a rifle across his knees.

You will see his knowledge of the subject and the enthusiasm of David in the following pages and I commend his book to you.

Sutherland

2012.

Chapter One

The Hunter's Horn

MY FATHER WAS a well beloved country parson. He also had the heart of a hunter. During his life, he was a ferreter, rough shooter and game shot. He was an active otter hunter and a foot and car follower of foxhounds. He fished wherever there was fishing to be had. Had there been deer around him, he would have hunted them. He was also an excellent amateur naturalist, who could tell you the name of every bird, butterfly, flower and tree in his locality.

My father's patron and squire was the late, great Ronald Arthur Vestey, the pre-eminent merchant prince of his generation. "RAV", as he was widely known, took a strong interest in my sporting education and generously provided me with unlimited sporting opportunities that enabled me to fish, shoot and stalk from an early age. Others - farmers, game keepers and retired military men - also fostered my early and doubtless obvious enthusiasm for all forms of field sports and fishing.

So it was that by the time I was five or six years old, I had heard the hunter's horn loud and clear and, as I hear it down more than half a century, it sounds notes as sweet now as it did then. I do not know what makes a man a hunter. I can only affirm that I heard the hunter's horn at that early age and have, happily, had it ringing in my ears ever since unceasingly.

In the days of my childhood, there were few deer in Suffolk's Stour Valley, where we had our home. In fact I do not remember ever

1

seeing deer at all save in the vicinity of Ickworth Park near Bury St Edmunds. Then there really were no deer to be seen in the woods or fields and it was not possible to turn any out during hunting or shooting days' as there were none there. Nowadays it is uncommon to go a day in Suffolk without seeing either fallow, muntjac, red or roe deer and, perhaps, more than one of these species.

It was therefore not until I visited RAV's estate in Sutherland, Scotland that I became aware of deer at all. Although too young to go to the hill on my first visits there, the significance of red deer and deer stalking was evident to me and I was greatly excited by it.

There was a library in the Lodge, on the walls of which were hung the heads of selected red deer stags. I would spend ages counting the points on these heads and reading the inscriptions showing who had been the successful rifle (usually RAV) and on which part of the estate the beast had been culled. There was also a gun room, permeated with the distinctive odour of gun oil, and this was my favourite room in the Lodge. Here was all the kit needed for stalking. The panelled walls had hooks on them from which hung well used leather cased stalking telescopes- no doubt in those days made by Stewart and Ross. The cabinets had rifle rods, jags and brushes in them. There were rifle cartridge cases and stalking knives. In these first visits to Sutherland, I was absorbing the ethos of deer stalking and longing to be old enough, and have legs long enough, to go to the hill.

I was allowed to fish and remember long, happy days casting for salmon, sea trout and brown trout on the loch in front of the lodge, under the supervision of a retired stalker, John Sinclair. As he held the boat broadside on a drift, Sinclair's eyes roamed irresistibly over the hill. Frequently he would spy deer and would try to persuade my father to look at them, which father would rarely do because that would have involved him talking his eye off his fishing flies.

I was much more susceptible to Sinclair's persuasion and, having sharp young eyes, I soon grew adept at spotting the parcels of deer that grazed the slopes below the high tops of Suilven and Canisp. As we fished, Sinclair would speak of times passed when he had enjoyed his heyday as a deer stalker. "I mind of the time..." he was wont to say as he recalled some interesting incident from stalks he

2

had undertaken. Fishing and shooting were acceptable pursuits to John Sinclair but could not hold a candle to the pursuit of deer.

At that time the greatest of the several ghillies in Lochinver, perhaps in all of Sutherland, was one Charlie Ross. Charlie Ross was the most elegant of salmon fly casters and an intelligent and success-ful fisher. A brilliant shot, I saw him watching snipe fly away from him through their twists and turns before he shot them with metro-nomic accuracy at what appeared to be impossible distances. He rarely missed. Charlie was also a keen and expert deerstalker. He was my mentor and my hero. First, he taught me how to fish for salmon, and the fishing days I spent under his instruction were quite magical. He could be strict at times, particularly when I "offended" a would-be taking salmon by being over excited and snatching the fly out of it's mouth. His threat to take his stick to me after two such incidents in the same pool put a stop to that and to this day I never ever strike a taking salmon.

Inevitably, it was Charlie Ross who stoked the embers of my nascent interest in deer stalking. As our visit was early in the stalking season there were no men capable of or interested in stalking in the Lodge and no doubt it suited Charlie and his colleagues to take me out on the hill to escape the drudgery of a ghillie's work on the river. Whatever his motives, I went to the hill for the first time with him.

I can recall the day well enough because the thick, low mist that covered the hill never lifted and no stalking was possible. My day started with a visit to the target, a life size replica in steel of a red deer stag. My shots must have been satisfactory as we then set out from the target up the hill path towards Canisp. Although the mist was all enveloping, Charlie Ross expressed the hope that it would lift later on in the day. Our party comprised Charlie who led from the front, myself as the Rifle and two pony men, who led shaggy garrons, each of which had on a special deer saddle. I already knew one of these ponies, an awkward grey which went by the name of Star. My sister, who fancied herself as a horse rider had mounted Star bareback one Sunday afternoon, but not for long. No sooner was she on board than Star bucked her smartly over his head and it was fortunate the pony paddock was soft and soggy and ideal for absorbing her fall.

Later, Star was to achieve immortality as a result of his misbehaviour during the construction of a barrage at what was to be the bottom of a new salmon pool. This pool was designated to be the Laird's Pool in honour of RAV, and deservedly so as he had done so much to improve the river. However, it was not to be. During the construction process the stalking ponies were pressed into carting the materials required to build the dam. Star considered such labour to be too hard, too prolonged and generally beneath his dignity as the senior stalking pony on the estate. He persistently balked at the tasks he was allotted and made the jobs of the ghillies and stalkers really miserable. They became so demoralised by his obdurate misdemeanours and bloody minded behaviour that they began to refer to the new pool as the Star Pool. The name stuck and I believe the pool is still the Star Pool to this day.

On my first morning's stalking, Star soon made his presence felt. The stalking path wended it's way generally upwards, with- here and there- knolls that would in open weather have made spying points for the stalkers. Although nothing could be seen for more than a few yards, with the mist right down, Star stopped at each and every one of these knolls and would not move on until he had had a rest and a bite of grass. A shop steward amongst horses, he insisted on his right to time out even though no spying was possible. Eventually, Charlie Ross got him on the move by ostentatiously pretending to spy at each of the horse's halts.

I was entranced. The stalker and pony men were in their tweeds, and wore heavy hobnail hill shoes. The stalker carried the rifle in it's case and now and then the leather case of his glass bumped against the small of his back. There was the clip clop of the ponies and the occasional scrape as a hoof slipped on a stone. The men and the ponies that comprised the stalking party walked steadily upwards. I remember it as if it was yesterday. I recall how happy I was to be in a stalking party going to the hill.

We walked out for a couple of hours and then sat down to an early piece. Charlie Ross consoled me in my frustration by telling me of how in the previous season he had been out in similar conditions and had heard a stag roar nearby and coming closer. He recounted how his rifle had shot the stag at close range when it had appeared in front

4

of them. The rest of my day proved to be an anti-climax as the mist never cleared and we were forced to turn for home without ever leaving the pony path. However, even out in such hopeless conditions, I had been thrilled by my first taste of the Scottish stalking day.

I was taken out again a day or two later on the other side of the estate with a different stalker, and missed a stag- a long shot across a wide gully- which embarrassed me as that day our party was a large one.

Then, Charlie Ross, sensing the pressure I was under, told me the two of us would go out alone and that when I shot a stag, he would call up the pony man. I did not know how he would do that, the era being long before radios were in use on the hill. He and I duly set off for the high tops above the head of Loch Assynt and, again, I can remember that day very clearly, even though it is fifty years ago. The moderate wind blew steadily from the south west and the sun shone. Eventually, we spied and stalked two comatose stags that were lying in the heather. With consummate skill and care, Charlie got me in to a knoll that could be used as a firing point. The stags, completely unaware of our presence, lay facing us with only their heads and necks showing. Close in and opposite these two great beasts, I felt for the first time the excitement that flows from a successful stalk mingled with the apprehension that I now had to take the shot.

Instructed to shoot the nearer stag in the neck, I fired and his head fell forward into the heather. The second stag never moved and when Charlie asked me if I wanted to shoot it too, I declined the shot. Even at that young age, with my first stag newly dead in the heather, I wanted to savour the moment and to enjoy the excitement and satisfaction of stalk and shot.

After a few minutes we stood up and went forward to bleed and gralloch my stag. Charlie then solved the mystery of how he was going to call up the pony man. Walking forward until he reached the slopes above Loch Assynt he simply set fire to some rank heather which soon produced a column of dense smoke. This was soon seen by the pony man, who then led his pony up the hill to us to load up and recover the stag.

It was, I recall, getting towards evening by the time we came off the hill: deerstalker, rifle and pony man in a timeless trio. I was not to know it then but there would be many barren years before I stalked deer again. Through them all, and into the present day, I still hold dear the memories of those first stalking days with my Highland mentor, Charlie Ross. I also remember with gratitude RAV, whose generosity gave me the opportunity to try the sport of deerstalking. I look back with affection on a beloved father who handed me his hunter's horn.

Well, all that happened a long time ago well before I was twenty. For the next twenty years, I did not stalk at all, as I had neither means or the time to do so. I was busy making my way in life with my young family and my profession and so, sadly, missed out on what should have been prime years in a deerstalker's life. Indeed, had it not been for two chance incidents, I might never have become the deer man that I now am.

By the late 1980s deer were spreading to parts of East Anglia where they had not been seen before, including the Mid Suffolk locality in which I by then lived. One night, whilst I was driving home from a local shoot, a roe buck ran into the road and collided with the off side of my truck. I stopped and, on seeing it writhing in the road, shot him in the back of his head with my shotgun. As the animal appeared to be otherwise undamaged, I decided to take it home and eat it. A day or two later, I skinned and jointed the carcass, and in due course my family enjoyed some roast joints and stews from it. I found the whole process interesting. I discovered that buck had broken his neck, admired the head – a moderate six pointer – and found the gralloching, skinning and butchering manageable tasks. That unfortunate buck opened my eyes to the possibility of stalking others, and the second chance event to which I have referred above was to facilitate this.

At that time my eldest son, Toby, was acting as an assistant keeper on a sporting estate on the north coast of Scotland. He visited the late Colin Haygarth's well known gun shop at Dunnet Head where he viewed a second hand Bruno .243 calibre deerstalking rifle, and he persuaded me to buy it. I already had a firearms certificate for my .22 rimfire rifle so it was a simple matter to obtain a variation of this to enable me to acquire this deerstalking rifle. This acquisition was to transform the rest of my life, although perhaps fortunately I had no perception of this at the time.

As I would not have purchased this stalking rifle without my son's encouragement, I owe him. Had he not revived my early interest in deer and deerstalking, I doubt I would ever have taken it up again. As it is, the pursuit of deer has become the overwhelming enthusiasm of my life in field sports and one from which I have derived great pleasure. In reflecting on the first taste of it that I had, thanks to generous men of my father's generation, and on my return to it many years later at the instance of my son, I acknowledge myself to be doubly blessed. I am also glad to record that in the years since the acquisition of my deer rifle, my son has developed his own deerstalking interests alongside mine and is now an accomplished, successful deerstalker..

Chapter Two

Starting Deer Stalking

A s I HAVE told it, I can, strictly speaking, claim to have started deerstalking as a youth in Scotland. However, my experience was so brief and so much was done for me that, with the arrival of my new rifle, I felt I was starting from scratch, and that I had a whole new sporting pursuit to learn. I set about my education with enthusiasm. First, I read what books I could find on deerstalking, with particularly close attention to those on roe deer stalking. Roe were the most obviously numerous species in my locality.

I read and, now and then still revisit, Richard Prior's instructive books on roe deer stalking. Whilst I like to think I would have found my own way to responsible stalking, Richard Prior's approach and ethics were so obviously correct and proper that it was easy to adopt them. He helped me to interpret the sightings I had of roe deer and their behaviour. His descriptions were short cuts for me towards an understanding of their behaviour in different wind and weather conditions and in their appetite for wild and cultivated crops in their season.

I learned to look for and recognise deer damage to forestry and crops and learned enough to be able to advise farm and forestry owners on this subject.

On taking deerstalking, as I was soon to do, it became second nature for me to census the deer population and design a deer management plan. Learning something also from Prior's pragmatism, I didn't and don't stick slavishly to the plan. There's many a slip between it's design and implementation. I soon discovered that now and then a deer that had too high a profile needed shooting and that this was about allaying the worries of the farmer and had nothing whatsoever to do with my cull plan.

Above all, at starting, I was naturally most concerned with the safety aspects of low ground deerstalking. At starting, I was very reluctant to take a shot other than from a high seat and even from an elevated perch I was wary about taking long shots on flat ground because of the shallow angle of the bullet's trajectory. As it happened, I was able to purchase an excellent lean to high seat, which was really well designed and constructed, and was in three sections. All these years later that high seat is still in regular use and has been an aid to the shooting of many deer. It was some years before I acquired the confidence and experience to regularly essay appropriate shots from ground level, perhaps using sticks for a lean or by shooting off a bipod. In those early days I undoubtedly passed up many opportunities that I would now take, but the important point is that I came through my apprenticeship without putting anyone else in danger.

Another preoccupation was with the technical aspects of deer stalking equipment. For instance, my first binoculars were a bulky Russian pair selected from, well, the bottom end of the market. In truth, they were not bad, but their shortcomings only became apparent to me when I purchased some 7 x 42 German binoculars and began to appreciate the benefits of having binoculars which excel at first and last light. Since then I have acquired two more pairs of binoculars manufactured in Germany. One of these pairs, in 8 x 56 is heavy and bulky, but superlative in low light conditions. In my opinion they were and are the ultimate binoculars for fallow deer stalkers, because of the crepuscular propensities of that species. I also own a nifty pair of 10 x 40 binoculars that fit nicely into the top pocket of most stalking shirts and are ideal for summer time forays after roe and muntjac deer.

I have usually favoured German products for stalking riflescopes too, and on the few occasions that I have economised I have been disappointed. For instance, when I wanted an illuminated scope I was offered a second hand scope for reasonable money. I got a reasonable scope but the lack of clarity compared with my high quality German scopes cancelled out the advantage of the illumination and, of course, on my turning up the magnification the haze increased so that it soon became impossible to get a bead on a beast. I have habitually used German optics, and will continue to do so until I can source optics from other manufacturers s of equal quality and lower price.

Although I anticipated mainly being a low ground stalker, I was also determined to stalk on the open hill in Scotland again and, at an early stage, I purchased a traditional three draw deer stalker's telescope from Greys of Inverness. I don't use it everyday but find it useful for identifying low and high ground roe bucks in season and for traditional red stag stalking. I have never regretted the considerable cost of my "glass" as it is called by highland hill deerstalkers.

I have put optics before rifles in my summary of stalking equipment to stress their relative importance. From my first forays, I recognised that far more time was spent by the deer stalker using his binoculars to observe deer than is ever spent aiming through his rifle scope. I would also aver that far more pleasure is derived from the use of the optics than it is from the firearm.

Turning now to rifles, I started with a basic .243 and then, wanting to stalk red deer stags, had custom made for me a .270. This rifle was built round a Sako action with a heavy, match barrel and a thumb hole laminated stock. It was accurate, and so heavy that it stayed rock steady on the hill in the strongest of highland gales. It was also excessively heavy to carry and deploy, and I kept it far too long before I sold it. Many years on, I currently have two rifles for deer stalking. First, my working rifle is a stainless steel lightweight 25.06 which I generally use with a moderator. This is my working rifle which I use almost every day during the winter doe cull. Flat shooting, with little recoil, it's a good tool for fallow deer doe culling, although in my opinion it's a bit strong for roe deer and muntjac.

My summer rifle is a 6.5 x 55 by Sauer, and it's my pride and joy. The calibre is naturally sweet shooting, and my rifle is a pleasing, beautiful example of it. This is my rifle of choice against roe bucks and muntjac in the spring and summer months.

When I started low ground deerstalking, the use of sound moderators was unusual. The police in the U.K. were then deeply opposed to them, presumably on the suspicion that a sound moderated centre fire rifle could and perhaps would be used as a sniper's weapon, although assassination by stalking rifle, moderated or not, is rarely if ever deployed in this country. Other grounds of opposition to them included one on purported safety grounds. The police suggested in this context that sound moderated rifles would be dangerous because members of the public would be unable to hear the shots and would be more likely to walk into the danger area. This absurd objection presupposed that the deer stalker would be splattering the bushes with multiple bullets, perhaps with automatic fire, rather than taking the usual single shot into a deer which would likely have a safe background behind it.

That attitude was thankfully abandoned several years ago and it is now routine to see a deerstalker with a "can" of one make or another on the muzzle of his rifle. The police now accept the health and safety argument- that the sound suppression protects the hearing of the deer stalker- and allow sound moderators on deerstalking rifles. With the increasing number of urban people living in the countryside, who complain about the noise of firearms when they are not complaining about other rural noises, there now seems a distinct possibility that the use of them may be made compulsory. Should this happen, deerstalkers will have seen the official police position move from prohibition to compulsion within two decades.

Another area of development is in deerstalking sticks. When I started, if deerstalkers used sticks at all, their choice was generally a single stout ash or hazel stick. A minority of deer stalkers used two sticks, joined by a strong band of rubber or a coach bolt six inches or so from their tops, which could be opened out to form a bipod. With woodland stalkers taking most of their shots from a standing position, the single stick was a basic aid to accuracy, with the bipod being even more effective in this respect and enabling the deer stalker to engage deer at longer ranges than had hitherto been the case. Now, of course, the majority of deer stalkers acquire the lightweight alloy, extending bipod sticks, which can be deployed at a range of lengths from 2′6″ to 5′6″ depending on whether the user is sitting, kneeling or standing and whether he is on flat or uneven ground. The latest deerstalking sticks have three or, in some cases, four legs and there seems to be no limit to the ingenuity of manufacturers in providing for the burgeoning deerstalking market.

In my early deerstalking days, I of course acquired the necessary equipment, the accessories to the essential rifle, scope, binoculars and stick. I purchased various knives and soon discarded most of the cheaper ones. I soon learned the importance of keeping my knives sharp and found that having a high quality steel blade was the best way to achieve this. Some blades would never keep an edge.

I became so interested in sharp knives that I splashed out on an expensive American made knife grinding machine, and took a training course on how to use it safely and to good effect. This machine was remarkably effective. After a little practice, I could achieve a really sharp edge on almost any knife with just a few passes through the grinding wheels at different settings. As with most products, high quality blades responded better to grinding than cheap ones. I still have this machine and use it regularly in my knife sharpening sessions.

In gralloching deer I found that the quickest way to blunt a sharp knife was to cut through deer hair with it. In order to decapitate a deer, I make a small incision in the neck and then cut through the skin from the inside thus avoiding the hair. During larder work my practice is to use one blade for cutting in or around bone and another for cutting soft tissue parts of the carcass.

Other items such as roe slings and sacks, drag ropes, roe and fox calls, and deer handling equipment were gradually acquired, some of which were to become useful and others which rarely made it off the gunroom shelf. Amongst this kit was the sturdy steel three piece high seat I have mentioned, brilliantly designed and engineered by a local man.

So it was that having armed myself with a serviceable .243 rifle and all the accessories, I was, like all novice deerstalkers, determined to shoot a deer.

Chapter Three

My First Roe Buck

AT THE BEGINNING of my low ground deerstalking career I lacked a mentor and had to progress as best I could by gaining practical experience. Having used a .22 rim fire rifle – the ricochet round– I was acutely aware of the inherent danger in discharging a full bore rifle. I started practising with my .243 in discreet places where the lie of the land enabled me to shoot into a hillside or bank without danger to any other person. I soon found my new rifle shot an accurate group and resolved to move on to the real thing. At that time I had no stalking of my own, but lived on an estate, the fields and woods of which were around my home. Roe deer were then to be seen from the first floor windows of my house, sometimes out in the open fields and more often on the woodland edge.

One particular roe buck was regularly to be seen either at the wood's edge or out on the swathes of rape. I watched this buck for sometime and was kindly given permission to shoot him by the estate's gamekeeper, who was responsible for controlling it's deer population. I was not given any instructions as to how I should achieve this task and was left to devise my own plan. The main problem was that the wood and rape field which the buck favoured formed a rectangle of flat land with public roads on all four sides.

These features made me to decide to erect my high seat on the edge of the wood overlooking the rape field. I hoped to catch the buck either leaving or returning to his home wood in the early hours of a July morning, before many people or vehicles were abroad.

At that stage, I had never previously erected my new high seat and, in the course of doing so on the woodland edge, soon learnt that there is a lot more involved in the effective positioning of a high seat than tying it to a tree. In fact, I found that wherever I put it, my view was obscured by branches from the tree and those adjoining it. I discovered that with a straight wood edge and the trees in full summer foliage, I had to secure my high seat to a tree with at least some visibility and then do some judicious pruning of various branches and twigs. I was rather apprehensive about lopping and pruning sufficient branches to win myself a clear field of fire. The pruning task didn't end with the branches immediately next to the high seat as, here and there along the woodland's edge, the view would be obscured or masked by overhanging branches and leaves and I painstakingly lopped as many of these as I could. At last I had a secure seat, with the benefit of views along the woodland edge and, in front, out over the large, swathed rape field.

The next morning I rose early and before dawn broke was sitting up in my high seat keenly awaiting the coming of the light. Long before that happened I was sweeping the woodland edge and field with my binoculars and learnt from this that what may be assumed to be dark is rarely pitch black. From a high seat, it's often the case, as it was that morning, that there is some visibility and this was accentuated by the light colour of the swathed rape crop and it's stubble. I sat in the high seat for an hour and a half and experienced for the first time the coming of the light and the change in the colours from mono to multichrome. As the light improved, and the colour seeped into the vista before me, I experienced great pleasure and happiness from watching it. Before I ever saw the buck, I felt quite clearly I was at a significant point in my life.

And I did see the buck. I spotted him as he emerged at the far end of the wood and prowled with some purpose along the headland that ran away to my front right. I recognised him as the buck I had previously viewed. He was the buck I wanted to shoot. He did not come within range of my rifle and went further way from where I first saw him in a determined manner until, to my chagrin, he disappeared entirely from view.

After he had gone out of sight, I continued to wait in the hope rather than the expectation that he would return. I did not really expect him to do so, having come to the view that he had likely made his way to an old pit in the next field surrounded by standing crops, and that he would lie up there for the whole day. I stayed on, but with little commitment. It seemed I would not get a chance that morning and that would be really disappointing because I was as keen as mustard to account for my first roe buck. In spite of these misgivings I continued to wait and, whilst I did so, the sun rose and began to flood the field in front of me with light and colour. I was struck by the way in which this changed the spectacle and enable me to identify objects that had previously been blurred or invisible. Then, as I watched, the sweep of my binoculars was arrested by some movement on the far side of the field. I concentrated on this area and saw it again, and that it was made by an animal bigger than a hare or rabbit, taller than a fox; it was a roe deer.

This deer was making it's way to the wood behind me and, in so doing, was approaching and likely to pass close by my high seat. I studied the animal through my binoculars, observing the way he was prowling confidently across the stubble and swathes. By then it was evident this was the buck that I had seen leave the wood at first light, and that he was returning to lie up for the day in the wood.

In the time since he had gone out into the fields, I had made, or so it seemed, hundreds of sweeps with my binoculars, and had altogether passed nearly three hours in fruitless observation. Now my time had come. With considerable feelings of excitement, I picked up my rifle which had been resting on the angle of the front and side rails of the high seat. I positioned the butt of the stock against my shoulder and, keeping my movements to a minimum to avoid scaring the buck, waited for him to come close enough to shoot. He came on, until I could clearly see the six points on his racks and his fox red summer coat and, when he stood clear of the rape swathes, his pizzle.

From his demeanour, I could sense that he was as confident of his status thereabouts as a regimental sergeant major on his own parade ground. Underneath his red coat his muscles rippled and I formed the impression he was designed for aggression, for territory holding and for breeding.

When, at length, he had approached to within eighty yards of me, and was angling from left to right across my front, I leant forward over my rifle, resting my elbows on the side rails like arm rests. I found the back of the buck's foreleg and raised the rifle a touch until the point of aim was nearly half way up the body. The buck was still, head half raised; the moment was frozen in time. Taking in and holding a breath, I squeezed the trigger gently and, with the shot, shattered the peace of the summer morning. In the reverberations of the rifle shot, the roe buck lunged forward towards the wood side, his legs paddling desperately until, after twenty yards, he collapsed and lay still in the stubble.

I reloaded my rifle and waited for a few minutes. I had read somewhere that one should do this. Waiting was difficult, as I was impatient to get to my buck. When I could stand it no longer, I got down and walked across the field to the spot where I thought I would find him. A minor panic then as he was not there, and everything- the stubble and the swathes of rape- looked different from ground level than they had when I was twelve feet above the ground level. I cast around and soon found my buck- I had underestimated the distance he was from me- and experienced a strong mixture of emotions. These included relief that I had shot my buck efficiently, excitement at my achievement and regret that I had taken the life of this magnificent animal. These are feelings I still experience to some measure with each beast that I shoot.

On a practical level, that morning, I found myself standing over the roe buck which I had shot, and with which I now had to deal. Since then I have gralloched many hundreds of deer of various species, but this was to be my first, apart from the victim of the collision with my car. I dragged my buck to the wood edge and set to work with the monstrous knife I then favoured. I shudder to think of the mess I made of that carcass, hacking away at it whilst trying to remember the guidance in Richard Prior's book. What had seemed so simple in his clear text, was much more tricky in the field. Eventually, I got the job done in an amateurish manner and had to solve my next problem, which was how to get the roe buck back to my vehicle. I did not have a roe sac then, but had recently acquired a roe carrier. It took me sometime to work out how best to attach the carcass of the buck to the four leather straps and how to shoulder it in a reasonably comfortable manner. That of course was a feature of starting stalking; everything I did took a while to do. Eventually, I recovered that buck and returned home with it as an exceptionally happy man.

My first morning's low ground stalking had convinced me that here was a wonderful pursuit that would obsess me for the rest of my life. Quite different from any other branches of the shooting sports of which I was an adherent- and there was a wide range of these- I was fascinated by every aspect of stalking. Also, and rather to my surprise, I was not bored by the long wait in the high seat which I had experienced in my first outing. Indeed, the outcome tended to show that in deer stalking, all things come to him who waits.

Having accounted for my first roe buck, I knew that I not only wanted to become a serious deerstalker but also that I wanted to do a lot of it. I now had an appetite for it that needed to be satisfied, and wanted to obtain my own deerstalking so that I could go out as and when I wanted.

Chapter Four

Bourn Valley Farms

A T THAT TIME, I was involved with a small shooting syndicate
close to my home and it occurred to me that no one was
stalking the deer there. It was only a small farm, with one or
two belts and the odd spinney and there were not a lot of deer there.
However, on the basis that this would be a start, I sought and
obtained permission to shoot deer there. Within the next year or two
the syndicate expanded it's land holdings by acquiring the shooting
rights over two more farms. I acquired additional deerstalking rights
over these too. By the time another year or two had passed, I had
obtained further rights over two more blocks of land that squared
off my holding and gave me access to not only more agricultural land
but also several small woods, plantations, belts and thick hedges.

In a relatively short period of years, I had put together a viable
deerstalking unit from five separate farms, an area altogether in
excess of fifteen hundred acres and with a good variety of terrain.
Cover for the deer was provided by the woods and plantations, some
of which were in the thicket stage. Feed was available in season in
the arable fields, and in various game covers sown every summer by
the shooting syndicate for the purpose of holding and driving our
game birds. A small stream or winter bourn runs through the land,
which, for convenience, from this point I will refer to as Bourn Valley
Farms. This stream was and is often quite clear and fast flowing in
winter but in high summer is often reduced to small pools of near
still water. It provides water for the deer the whole year and the

banks of it were also greatly favoured for the herbs and sweet grass on which the deer like to graze.

Having a block of this size under my control, I was able to take a proactive view of the deer and my intended culls. I was able to census the population annually and from the start make recommendations to my farmer owners as to how many and which age and gender groups of deer should be culled. Thus, with just a little help from Richard Prior's book, I adopted a methodology that I have adhered to ever since: counting, planning, recommending and actioning. Although my culls have varied from year to year the usual roe cull is five roe bucks and five roe does. Muntjac are shot on sight subject to the standard recommendations as to only shooting yearling or obviously pregnant muntjac does. Fallow are more frequent in adjoining areas than they once were but the odd visitor that falls to my rifle is almost invariably a wandering pricket. I would not be popular if I allowed fallow to become residents on the Bourn Valley Farms. I have been managing the deer on the Bourn Valley Farms for many years now and have found that this approach is acceptable to my farmer landowners and also to the majority of the local population, many of whom walk the public footpaths that exist over some of the land. I should add a minority of these walkers trespass wherever they wish which creates significant issues as to safety and disturbance.

At the start, the deer on the Bourn Valley Farms were exclusively roe, and as such quite easily managed. Subsequently, the farms were colonised by muntjac. At the time of writing more fallow visit than was ever the case in the early days, although none of these take up permanent residence in my small woods. The muntjac population is more difficult to control than the roe and, every year, the occasional fallow culled are encountered more by chance than design. Their presence is so ephemeral that it's rarely productive to set out one's stall for them.

As I was already involved in the Bourn Valley Farms pheasant shoot, I was familiar with much of the ground, particularly during the winter months. When I became a deerstalker, I started visiting regularly throughout the year and had the pleasure of enjoying the land in it's summer livery. I soon learned that the prime spring months for roe buck stalking were April and May, and that by the beginning of June the cover was so extensive and tall that effective stalking is impossible. I experienced for the first time the unsurpassable pleasure of low ground deer stalking in mid or late May and the associated and less welcome impact on the deerstalker's mental faculties from frequently rising at 3 and 4 a.m. for a pre dawn start. I found then and still find myself now enthralled by being out for a prowl in the fields and woods before others are abroad and, perchance, to cull a roe buck and finish the morning outing by basking for a few minutes in the warm early summer sunshine on a comfortable grassy bank.

Always aware that every farm has it's politics as well as it's geography, I have generally found my farmer "clients" to be practical chaps who, having entrusted me with the management of their deer, have let me get on with the job. I found out early on find they want to know the facts and figures of the cull, but not the war stories and incidents of my deerstalking. As far as they are concerned, I am there to do a job and keep "deer numbers down".

On the whole gamekeepers are tolerant too, notwithstanding their reputation to the contrary. On Bourne Valley Farms, I have worked happily for a number of years alongside it's gamekeeper and, I hope, helped him by finding fox dens, shooting foxes and reporting the movements of trespassers. Over the years, the only trouble I have ever experienced has invariably been caused by the occasional amateur game keeper with an attitude best described by the phrase: "The woods belong to me!" I recall one of these pulled down my high seats and threw them in a pond. Happily, it was not long before he was thrown off the land, which brought to an end his attempts at being a gamekeeper. For some years afterwards, I would see this fellow walking his dogs on and off public footpaths. For all his boorish behaviour whilst he was playing at being a gamekeeper, he became an habitual trespasser on other people's land. I observed him more than once furtively checking whether the coast was clear before departing from the public footpath and walking over the fields, with his unruly dogs flushing and chasing any game they encountered. On occasion, he passed in front of my high seat and never saw me watching him. I found this amusing.

Parts of Bourn Valley Farms are heavily walked and some of the walkers are prone to trespass off the public rights of way. On one of the farms, a permissive path allowed by the landowner through the middle of the farm is used more as a stepping off path than a walk in itself. This is an abuse of the owner's generosity in granting the permissive status. As the responsible deer manager on the land, I have had to assess the risks arising from both the public rights of way and the trespassing public. The latter are a constant menace from a safety point of view. They are also disruptive of the deerstalking process and it's all too frequent that some "off limits" individual wrecks my morning or evening outing.

I have challenged a number of these characters over the years and in response they variously threaten violence, particularly if they are in the company of a female, use abusive language, make pathetic excuses or claim some tenuous permission for being on private land. However, by observing and studying the furtive way they behave I have no doubt at all most of them know they are trespassing and are just hoping to get away with it.

One summer morning, whilst it was still dark, I approached the bourn with a view to sitting on it's edge overlooking the grass meadow and woodland edge on the far side of it. In the corner of this was a hummock which deer were and are fond of using to survey the meadow before they leave the security of the trees. On this particular morning, I saw what appeared to be a beast just in front of this and watched it carefully for some minutes whilst waiting for the shooting light to come. Whilst waiting, I decided the beast did not seem quite right and, when there was sufficient light to see, what I saw was not a deer at all. It was a motor cycle behind which was pitched a small tent. Had I engaged it, that would have made a rare trophy!

Another early morning, whilst walking into one of the woods with a view to sitting up in a high seat, I encountered a man who claimed to be an ornithologist heading in the same direction. Whilst I was digesting this information, and the fact that I might easily have found myself stalking the wood at first light without knowing he was there, he told me not to look so worried and disappeared into the wood. Apparently, he had permission to be there on that occasion, but a farm manager had left me out of the loop. Another evening, I turned up to find a farm walk in progress. On both occasions, I changed my plan and stalked elsewhere.

Another incident turned out to be quite amusing. I was sitting in a high seat in a wood in which the compartments were laid out in rectangular blocks divided by mown rides. My seat was on one cross roads and eighty yards in front of me was another. At last light, what looked at first sight like a fallow pricket appeared on this other cross roads followed by a man with a dog. The first animal was a huge wolf hound or similar breed on an extending lead. The man and dogs crossed left to right and disappeared out of sight. Very quickly, and quite independently of them, a muntjac buck appeared on the ride immediately to my left. I engaged it and, a few seconds after the report of the shot, the man and his dogs fairly scuttled back they way they had come. That was the last time I saw him in that wood! I would add that my shot was a perfectly safe one being directed away from him. At the time I was very upset by his unauthorised presence, and for him potentially introducing hazard into a culling situation which I had designed to reduce risk.

One summer evening I was enjoying the late evening sunshine in one of my favourite high seats when a car was driven through a gateway opposite me into the field I was watching. The driver parked it against the hedge and, in short order, a man and woman got out and engaged in a brief, frantic sexual tryst. As soon as they had finished they jumped back into the car and went off. I will leave it to readers' imaginations as to where I looked whilst this was on going.

I have come to regard the presence of members of the public, wherever they turn up, as part of the politics of my stalking ground. I can do nothing to deter those who walk on public rights of way and very little more to prevent trespassing by those who do not respect private land. This latter grouping make my culling assignments potentially more hazardous than they would be if I knew persons would stay on designated routes, but is a feature that I have to weave my way around. Low ground deer live in close proximity to humans whose presence, welcome or not to the deerstalker, is inevitable.

Chapter Five

Some Interesting Stalks

T HE MAJORITY OF the fields on the Bourn Valley Farms were and are large and open and so a direct approach is rarely advisable, especially in the spring and winter months when there is little crop or other vegetation to conceal the deer stalker. So it was that on that early April morning, with a bitterly cold wind gusting in from the North, I started in from the south side of my ground and made what use I could of the hedges and ditches to supplement the cover provided by the pre- dawn darkness. Stopping now and then to spy, I made my way from the farm by following the track eastwards which was concealed for the first three hundred yards by a hedge either side of it. Then, where I had to turn north, I had a hedge to my left and kept close to this, only pausing to glass the field on the far side of it at the one convenient gap. At the end of this hedge was another little used track, which made a sort of T-Junction with it and went away north east, following the gentle drop in the gradient until it reached the bourn in the bottom of the valley.

The light was coming fast now and the blackness of the previous few minutes was being modified by the grey dawn shades. I had my rifle on my shoulder, my binoculars to my eyes and was trembling with a mixture of cold and excitement. I paused for some minutes on the T-Junction glassing intently to my left where there was something of a small but heavily overgrown spinney. I also swept the open fields to the north although with little expectation of seeing deer on them in such a biting wind. At length, when satisfied there were no beasts in my immediate vicinity, I turned to my right and stalked the hedge and derelict track that led to the watercourse.

I knew from previous experience that just because I had not seen any deer, I could and should not assume there were none there. I knew it was easy for a beast to lie hidden in the bottom of the hedge on the ditch bank and, unless winded, only jump up and make off when it became aware of me coming close to it. With this risk in mind, I went very cautiously. If there was a beast there, it was likely all I would see of it would be an ear or an antler. After a careful but unrewarded stalk, I reached the bourn. In summertime, the grass and vegetation grows high enough on it's banks to conceal a stalker but that cold morning in April there was no such cover. The bourn was running fast and clear between it's steep banks and there was no option for me other than to slide down one side of these and use the bed of the bourn to stalk into the grass at the bottom of Black Wood.

In wellington boots, I could negotiate my way along the stream bed in most places but here and there, when I came to the deeper places and small pools I had to move to one side or the other and edge along half in and half out of the water all the while trying to keep my head below the top of the banks. I was familiar with this stalk, having negotiated the stream bed several times, and used certain strategic bends to put my head up cautiously up and glass the fields through which it ran. I saw nothing, and the wind was chill. After persisting in my approach for several hundred yards, I came to a stoway which enabled the tractors and farm machinery to cross the bourn. This was built over a big pipe through which the whole stream flowed. Today the pipe was three quarter full and I smiled at the recollection I had of crawling through it to get into a parcel of does that had been grazing out in the open one afternoon. I would not be doing that this morning. Instead, I checked the coast was clear and then climbed up and crawled across the bare tracked stoway, and then dropped down again into the watercourse on the downstream side. A further paddle downstream took me to a convenient stand of blackthorn which gave on to both the grass pasture below Black Wood and the sheltered south side of it. It was a spot of strategic importance and I crawled into the cover at the bottom of it, and settled myself as best I could to wait on what if any deer might appear.

I do not know what other deerstalkers think about whilst waiting in ambush for deer, but I have a tendency towards uncertainty and ambivalence that can cause me to become impatient. On that morning, I was bothered by the cold wind. It was not that I minded it myself, although I could feel it keenly enough. It was rather that I began to convince myself that deer would simply stay tucked up in the warmest spot they could find and would not move at all until much later in the day when, perhaps, the sun would come out. I was also uncomfortable, absorbing cold from the ground and painful pricks from the blackthorn every time I moved. It took some will power to wait on in the hope, and it was more a hope than an expectation, that a cull roe buck would show.

I knew from being out doing my doe cull that there were at least two little cull bucks in Black Wood, and that on an ordinary morning's outing I ought to se at least one of them. However, as the cold and the discomfort affected me, I became more and more despondent about my chances. Having been out on the ground since 4.45 a.m. I had stalked for approaching three hours without seeing an ear. I kept looking and checking as I set myself target times to remain where I was, telling myself that this corner place gave me a double chance as I might see a buck either on the meadow or up the wood side. The thought of the cold wind on the far side of the wood reduced the odds on my buck venturing out that way and increased my chances still further.

Even so, I was within a minute or two of moving on when I caught sight of a movement high up the south side of the wood. A moment's glass work with my binoculars revealed the grey coat of a winter coated roe deer. It was half in and half out of the woodland edge, and only when it stepped out and lifted it's head could I confirm it was one of my cull bucks. I had an immediate decision to make. I had to decide whether to stay where I was and hope the buck would come down the hill and give me a shot or to put a stalk in on him. Knowing that the ground flattened off at the top of the wood, I decided to stay where I was. In consequence, I had a nerve wracking half hour. The young buck worked his way down the wood edge, sometimes outside and at others just inside the woodland margin. Each time he disappeared, I tended to think he had gone for good and that I should have got up and gone after him.

Those were in fact just the thoughts I was having when he reappeared for the last time eighty yards uphill from my position and presented a perfect broadside shot. I raised my stalking sticks, that I had reduced to their shortest height on reaching the ambush site earlier. I rested the rifle in the fork of them and found the point I wanted just an inch behind the left foreleg. I squeezed the trigger gently. The roe buck lurched forward five or six yards and collapsed on the grass. I reloaded and waited for a few minutes watching the fallen buck for any signs of life but there were none. He had been killed instantaneously.

When I walked forward to inspect the carcass, I noticed the scruffy winter coat already coming away in places in anticipation of the change to his summer pelage. I observed the so slight disturbance at the point of entry of the bullet. The head had thin four point racks and the body size appeared lightweight. Using my drag rope, which I attached round his neck, I dragged the beast over the grass to the edge of the bourn and made ready to gralloch him.

Coat off and sleeves rolled up to keep them clean of blood, I placed the beast on the flat top of the bank before starting the gralloch. I hurdled the back legs and carefully opened up the beast before moving him so that he was lying on the slope of the bank and I could use gravity to help eviscerate him and remove all the green and red pluck and the contents of his back passage. Then, using a small cloth I carry, I was able to sponge the inside of the rib area, making for a beautifully finished carcass. There was a mature willow tree handy so I hung the buck's carcass on a convenient branch to drip and dry. Then, dropping down into the stream bed, I washed my hands and arms and also my knives and saw. Water and wind were both keenly chill so it was good to get my coat back on and take a brisk walk back to my vehicle with a view to collecting the carcass.

As always, after an early morning outing, the countryside, whilst still lovely, had lost it's post dawn drama. The ground game, so apparent first thing, seemed to have made itself scarce. The stables by the farm were busy with equine activity and a tractor was already at work out of sight. The unwelcome sound of traffic on the main road was to be heard together with other noises of the human kind. It was as if I had walked out of an enchanted garden and, as I had and have done so many times before and since, I felt delight for being a deerstalker.

I have recounted above how on that particular April morning, I stalked in from the south side of my ground, and how I worked the wind blowing in from the north. A south or south westerly was and is my prevailing wind and of course required an altogether different approach. There is a lane that runs through the middle of my ground, and the route of this is approximately six hundred yards and two fields distance from the north side of Black Wood. The lane itself is heavily wooded and, as Black Wood lies on lower ground it cannot be seen from it. However, if the deerstalker leaves his vehicle by the roadside and walks directly over the crest of the hill, he at once comes into the view of any deer in or even in the vicinity of the wood. My early efforts at getting into Black Wood were abject failures and I learnt the hard way the truth in the aphorism that "experience is the name men give to their mistakes".

As the problems set by the geography of this section of my stalking ground are similar to those on other land, I shall describe them. The land comprised a rectangle, the north side being the lane and the south side Black Wood. To the west, and at a slightly lower level was a big wood and to the east were flatter open fields. Two hundred yards in from the east and west boundaries of the rectangle were two smaller woods. At times roe deer were to be encountered in any of these features including the hawthorn, tree studded hedges that ran between them.

My abortive attempts to get into this ground were quite different. Walking straight in- taking a direct route- through the middle resulted in my bumping deer in the crops, if there were any or even spooking deer in the wood if there were not. I know this happened; I sometimes saw them running out…An approach down the west flank resulted in me showing myself to the deer within the big wood there and I noted that after that approach I would never during the rest of the outing see deer coming into my killing field from the west. The approach off the east flank had the benefit of cover from a respectable hedge, but the disadvantage of being open to view from the middle of the ground. Unless there was a deer in or about the hedge that was a dead end approach.

There was one possible approach that would sometimes work. It was the option I adopted one early May morning. I was on the ground by 4.30a.m. and, having parked my truck by the side of the road, I walked along it, well hidden by the hedge, before tiptoeing around the new barn conversion that was at that time owned and occupied by a charming local farmer. Agreeable as he was, I didn't want to rouse him or his sheep dogs at that hour of the morning, and was much relieved when I had bypassed his place and was heading in an easterly direction through a shallow swale at the end of his extended lawn. After five minutes walk, I turned to the south and began to walk towards Black Wood, using as cover the hedge now in front of me and the most easterly of the two small woods. I could only use the latter as cover for part of the walk as it was as likely to be occupied by deer at that time of day as Black Wood itself. Having got within a hundred yards of it, I moved right handed and relied on the hedge for cover.

That morning luck was with me and I made it to the hedge where there was growing on the higher bank on my side a decent sized oak tree. I had previously dropped off a short ladder under this tree and also made improvements to it to facilitate a shot. These were a combination of judicious pruning and the addition of shooting rails to it's branches, which I had secured with ropes. On reaching this tree, I stood very still for several minutes but saw nothing move. I then leaned the ladder against the tree and climbed into the middle of it, from which I knew that I would, when the light properly came, have a great vantage point. I was I suppose seven feet above the ground on my side of the hedge and ditch and at least ten feet above the field before me the other side of which was the north side of Black Wood. I was aware that I would not only be able to see the wood in front of me but part of the meadow below it and the banks of the bourn. I would also be able to see much of the ground to my east and west including the small wood quite close to my tree.

Brimming with confidence, I sat in the oak tree and watched the scene as the light came. I watched the herons flying to and from the heronry, mobbed by crows. Early pigeons were beginning to fly after their night's roosting, hungry to fill their crops. A sparrow hawk flew low and fast from a branch in the hedge top, speeding across the drilled wheat to the corner of the field to the alarm of the small birds in the hedge rows. As the light improved pheasants appeared on the woodland edge and I could hear partridges calling. In the immediate vicinity of my tree top perch, I could hear and see small birds. The ubiquitous black bird was most common but for a few minutes a pair of wrens fluttered in the thorn bushes to my right singing their high pitched songs.

I kept as still as I could and continued to watch. At length, I spotted a roe deer walking along the hedge to the east- to my left- and studied it with the binoculars: a doe on her own. She disappeared from view into the top of Black Wood and, although I tried I could not see her again. It was, I realised, more than likely she was moving down the wood and would pass in front of me. Shortly after this, I saw another doe and follower slip out of the bottom of Black Wood and make their way quite quickly to the watercourse, which they crossed before disappearing out of my picture to the right.

Their rapid departure unnerved me. I wondered if I had somehow spooked them. After all, I had had several failed attempts at getting into this ground. I thought that perhaps they had seen me by the tree or heard an unnatural noise as I positioned the ladder and climbed into it. If that was the case, and I thought it must be, then that was immensely disappointing and all the more so as there really was no other position to which I could effectively move now that the light had come. I had to stay put but, with the departure of the two beasts, time dragged and, with my morale ebbing as fast as the light was improving, I sulked.

And then, faster than I can write these words, the buck was on the field. He could only have come out of the small wood to my east and was angling his way west across my frontage. He was a serious roe buck, big in body weight and straight across the back. His head was clean and I could see, I thought, six points. His coat was between summer and winter. As he crossed the drilled crop he paused now and then to graze and to check his surroundings.

As I overlooked him I assessed that buck for culling or sparing. I had, I knew, better bucks than him on my ground. Although he might improve, he was surplus to requirements and I feared that he would displace my big six pointer before his time was up and those concerns made up my mind for me. Taking a lean off my new rail, I waited for the buck to move round into my killing zone and, when he duly did, the shot that killed him, destroyed the top half of his heart. I looked at him as he lay on the green wheat with a little sadness for he was a fine beast if not as good as my best. And then, carrying his considerable weight in my roe sac, I made my way back to the lane well satisfied with my morning. I had, through a mixture of ingenuity and preparatory work, overcome the difficulty of stalking that place. I had risen early and got in there before light. I had sat out my disappointment and taken my chance with a true, safe shot. I had culled a buck that needed culling.

The shooting of that buck from my oak tree hide caused me to become very fond of it and, in a south or south westerly wind, it became one of my favourite places from which to watch and wait for deer. It was, first, a discreet place being too far away from the roads and footpaths for most people although even there I encountered some trespassers. Secondly, the position allowed a near all-round view of the landscape with the best of these enabling me to look into the prime deer holding areas. I came to very much enjoy the spectacle that this provided. The landscape was a mixture of woodland and arable and in the valley there was the small bourn. There were always animals to watch and often deer. The bird life was varied with plenty of game birds which, as a shooting man involved with the local syndicate, I was always glad to see.

It was of course the deer that were my principal preoccupation. Concealed in my oak tree perch- on those mornings that I could access it without frightening a deer- I could watch and study the behaviour of the local deer in detail, to the point that I could identify some of them, and their family groups.

Although I had read of the regularity of roe deer and their propensity to turn up in the same place at the same time day after day, that was not on all fours with my observations.

At that time I had on the place a most distinctive master buck with a classic six point head. I liked to think of him as "the father of my herd" and relished seeing him usually in the company of his does.

As he was so distinctive I never had a problem in recognising him. However, he showed himself, if at all, in several different places. More than once he appeared from the small wood to my left on the field in front of the high seat, following the route back to Black Wood that I have described earlier. I saw him sometimes at the top of Black Wood, where he would spend some time marking what I supposed to be the boundary of his territory. On other mornings he would prowl along the bourn bank, stopping and dropping down now and then to graze on the sweet herbs that grew there in the damp soil.

Even a subtle shift of the wind would make him change his position and, until he became too hot he enjoyed wind sheltered sun warmed spots. His life appeared to consist of an early morning prowl around his territory, or parts of it, with the marking of boundaries at strategic points followed by lengthy periods of grazing, browsing and dozing. I much enjoyed monitoring this fine buck who illustrated that a roe buck always looks much better alive than he does dead.

Often this buck was in the company of does and I could only speculate as to whether he had mated the previous rut with one or more of these or, as I supposed, his mate was the old doe and the younger doe was one of his progeny. Now and then the old doe would rough up the young one, which supported my theory that she was, as it were, an unwelcome teen aged daughter hanging around the house.

The old doe was wary and it was amusing to watch her on the drilled wheat on such mornings as she chose to graze it. Her appearance on the wood edge was, I spotted once or twice, preceded by her standing just inside the wood and checking the fields outside for danger. She would, if satisfied, then emerge and make another check with eyes, ears and nose working overtime. Only if fully sure that there was no trouble about would she then start to graze, feeding into the wind as far as she could and punctuating her grazing with moments of observation when her head and neck would be rotated more like a snake than a mammal. In these movements she concealed some intense observation, the taking of the most prudent precautions and never raised her head unless she had cause for alarm. If I was lucky, she might lie down on the drill and we passed several pleasant interludes during which I was comfortably ensconced in my high

31

seat and the master buck and does enjoyed a doze in the early summer morning sunshine.

However, the daily life of roe deer is greatly affected and disturbed by people and long before breakfast time on a typical May morning what I came to think of as daytime noises would cause unease amongst the roe deer family. Invariably the old doe would be the first of them to unfold her limbs and stand. She would listen for the distant noises that had caught her attention and look round as if for confirmation that these were caused by man. Then she would look to the woodland cover and, after a few moments, walk back to it followed by the rest of the family. The buck would likely be the last to go in, visibly reluctant to abandon the grazing and sun sheltered spot in which he had been so comfortably couched. Apart from my master buck and his immediate family there were of course other roe deer that I saw and, on occasion, shot from the oak tree high seat. In it's first year of use, the local roe buck population was high and I had and took several buck culling opportunities from this elevated position. At that early stage of my deerstalking career, I was very reluctant to shoot from ground level unless, say, I could shoot a deer standing on a hillside, when I could I hoped, assume the bullet and shrapnel from it would soon be earthed. This made the use of the elevation of the oak tree all the more attractive to me and I intensely enjoyed both watching and shooting from it, and felt particularly secure and safe whilst engaging roe deer on the field in front of it and as far as the wood's margin.

Chapter Six

Deer by Wet Places and Ponds

THERE IS ONE other feature of Black Wood I should perhaps mention and that is it's pond. From my oak tree high seat this was forward left of me and screened by willows. I noticed that deer often emerged from the vicinity of it or, if undisturbed outside the wood, naturally trekked back into the wood at that point. Plainly this was a feature that the roe deer liked. This realisation led me to examine the other wet places and ponds on the Bourn Valley Farms and to assess how useful they would be as deer culling places. I have already described the upstream part of the bourn and it's value both as a location favoured by the roe deer and, in their absence, as a discreet route into the bottom corner of Black Wood. Much further downstream, at the lower end of my ground, the bourn runs through ancient water meadows still used for grazing cattle stock in the summer season.

These meadows are enclosed by straggly hedges which, reinforced with barbed wire, are intended to be stock proof. The herbs and sweet grass that grows prolifically in these meadows are fancied by deer and I recognised this as a potential killing field. However, in practice, I encountered a snag never really resolved. The irregular shape of the meadows and the large number of overhanging branches made it all but impossible to position a high seat with a worthwhile field of view let alone fire. I had a free standing high seat but could not place this in the meadows because of the stock.

Having wasted a great deal of time trying to resolve this

apparently irresolvable problem, I took to stalking the meadows on foot and, if I encountered a regular beast, positioning a temporary high seat for the one chance this would provide. On one such occasion, I managed to secure my lean to high seat to the branches of a tall thorn bush in the perimeter hedge where I had twice seen a buck feeding. On my first evening here, the buck stepped out only forty yards to my left and I shot him. On examination, I found him to have a small bullet wound from what I would say was a .22 bullet in his left hind leg. This wound was swollen, smelly and puss filled. Apart from deriving some satisfaction from having culled an injured beast, this operation, with my temporary high seat being erected and the buck accounted for within the same day, was an object lesson in the importance of having the high seat in the vicinity of roe deer. The stalker can move the high seat to these deer; he cannot generally bring roe deer to the high seat.

Several other ponds on Bourn Valley Farms might ordinarily have proved attractive to both the roe deer and myself as the stalker but were spoiled by their proximity to public footpaths, roads, houses and farm buildings. One pond, probably an old bomb crater, was plainly attractive to roe deer as I would see them around it in the very early morning but it was situated in a flat, open place and only a few yards from a small settlement of houses. Noise disturbance and safety considerations- but not in that order – meant there was just nothing I could do with them. In any event, by the time shooting light came these visitors would be moving back to safer quieter parts of the farms.

Another two ponds, both visited by deer on occasion, presumably mainly during the hours of darkness, could not be exploited because they were beside a heavily walked permissive path. Had I erected a high seat beside this, one or more of the visiting walkers would no doubt have pulled it down and done what damage they could to it. And these were invitees not there on the path as of right!

In spite of these disappointing situations, there was a pond the surroundings of which lent themselves rather well to the placement of a permanent high seat. This had the great advantage that it could be approached discreetly from the back of some houses in the nearby village. Whilst this approach was best made in the dark, it was possible in low light as there was a great deal of overgrown cover, trees and bushes around the pond. On the side furthest from the village, the east facing side, the high seat overlooked a gently sloping field at the bottom of which was a reed bed with alder and willow trees and some box and yew, in all an attractive habitat for roe deer. One April I identified a suitable tree on this side of the pond and, after judicious pruning, was able to erect a high seat with excellent, extensive fields of view, with the latter being very safe. I called this the Village High Seat. I didn't know it at that time, but I was to spend many happy hours there over the future years.

My birthday fell on the 13th May and I was invited to meet a friend for lunch and an afternoon's dry fly fishing on East Anglia's premier chalk stream, the River Wissey. He explained that it would likely be too early for any mayfly, but that if we were lucky a few hawthorn flies might hatch. I couldn't care less what hatch there would be; I just wanted to be on the river bank. I greatly enjoyed fishing that river. As it was my birthday, and prime roe buck time, I decided to stalk first and prepared myself for a long day. The previous evening I made ready my stalking and fishing equipment and set the alarm clock for 4a.m. A prompt response to it's call meant that I got on to the ground in the dark and had time to make my way into my Village High Seat without being compromised.

There is always something very satisfying about settling into a high seat without (as far as one knows) disturbing any deer. No animals have rushed off into the darkness; no disturbed old doe is standing off and barking and nor are there any alarm calls. That's how it was that morning. I walked in, crept round the pond (a real danger area) and as quiet as a ghost climbed up the ladder to my perch, remembering for once to ensure my back did not move the wooden plank seat and cause it to bang against the metal supports or rails. I settled into the seat with the minimum of movement and shuffling, and rested the rifle on the angle formed by the left hand and front rails, with enough of the scope sight supported by the front rail to prevent it from twisting. Once settled, I composed myself and waited for the light to come.

In a morning outing the light is the deerstalker's friend. In the spring and early summer "she comes fast" and when she comes she

35

reveals to him the deer he pursues. That morning, I recollect, the light came quick. She stripped away the blanket of the night and revealed, on the grass before me, dark shapes. As she peeled away more darkness I could make out that these shapes were roe deer. I could not tell whether they were bucks or does and, even as I watched, they disappeared. In the improving light I was left overseeing an empty field.

I cannot tell you now how long I waited; I can only record that I felt the hunter's happiness at being out on the ground in the freshness of an early May morning. I felt the love of the chase, and the need to account for my quarry. These emotions were enhanced by the fly fishing treat ahead of me that afternoon and the chance of success with both rifle and rod in a single day. And as I thought on these things, a roe buck was on the field! One moment an empty paddock; the next a sward occupied by a purposeful buck. And he was coming, coming on to me, coming fast. I shouldered the rifle, judging the distance as he reduced it. I was counting it down, 350, 300, 250, 200 yards, and still he was coming, not running but coming on hard and with purpose. I wanted him in at the lone hawthorn bush, the bush with the browse line all round it and he came on, head facing me, and on reaching the bush turned far enough to present a broadside shot. I took it and he lunged and plunged and lay dead on the dewed grass. A birthday buck! My birthday buck!

I was home with him before the family were awake, and had done with him what deerstalkers have to do before they were dressed. My buck carcass was fly netted and hanging in the deer larder and I was making coffee before my wife came downstairs. "Did you get one?" she asked. "Yes I got one" I replied. And she heard the words, but not at all the haunting call of my hunter's horn.

Later that day, on the banks of the beautiful river, I watched a hatch of black hawthorn flies cause a good trout's rise. Creeping upstream on hands and knees, I cast my imitation hawthorn a yard above him and saw the black bodied white winged imitation fly alight. He took first cast and I netted him five minutes later: my first brown trout of the season. My friend returned and admired my fish. He supplied me with lunch and wine and toasted my anniversary. After lunch, I was sleepy and rested by the river. The sun came out and suddenly mayfly were hatching in myriad clouds. The big flies turned and spun intent only on their mesmeric dance and, I watched, as if in a trance, whilst the trout of the river rose to their chance. The surface of the stream rippled with their slashing, savage rises. Every lie held a feeding trout in frenzy.

The hunter in me wanted one, a big one and so I watched and stalked and cast for a heavy trout rising regularly by a vertical reed. The black hawthorn was back in my box and the big yellow partridge hackle mayfly was attached to my leader. Grease on the leader, flotant on the fly, I cast over the brown trout and he took savagely, was well hooked and then landed.

Later that day, as the last of the evening drained away, I reflected on my extraordinary good luck in life. My day, my birthday, had begun long before the public were abroad. My morning buck was accounted for before breakfast and the hours immediately before and after the top of that May day had been spent fly fishing on a beautiful river. My trophy brown trout completed the right and left of a fortunate fellow. As I reflected on that day I knew I would never sit up in the Village High Seat again without remembering the thrill of that birthday during which I had shot a roe buck and caught a brace of trophy brown trout. That memory still burns brightly!

I have mentioned how, in those days, I rarely engaged a beast on my ground unless I could do so from some sort of high seat, which enabled me to use the ground as a back stop. Even long, shallow angled shots from a high seat disturbed me as it seemed a bullet or some of the shrapnel from it was much more likely to ricochet from a flatter shot than from one at a sharper angle. My disinclination to shoot from ground level was based on the difficulty in getting a solid earth back stop and a lack of knowledge as to how a bullet behaves after hitting a deer, the earth or, indeed, any object that impedes or obstructs it's flight. I had read of bullets which had passed through the target deer and killed or wounded another standing well away from it, and apparently out of the line of fire. I have asked ballistics experts and other knowledgeable people about this without ever eliciting a satisfactory answer. The trouble is that no one knows the precise path of any particular bullet, although they may have a good notion of it's probable direction. In my early years as a low ground deer stalker, I kept myself out of trouble by adopting my self-imposed restriction of mainly engaging deer from high seats. I also always tried to keep in mind the aphorism that the whilst any fool can loose a bullet, the greatest genius in the world cannot recall it.

As a low ground deerstalker I wanted a bullet that would shoot flat to point of aim up to a distance of two hundred yards and would then stop. Having complained about the absence of such a missile, I have recently been informed that a great deal of research and development has been undertaken on behalf of the military for just such ammunition. If it succeeds, and such ammunition becomes available for sporting rifle shooting then I shall be a buyer, and most of my longstanding worries and concerns about making a dangerous shot will be almost entirely extinguished.

This was a subject that I thought about a lot whilst using my Village High Seat. Although deer sometimes came into range behind it, I could and in any event would not have fired back towards the village. To the front of the seat, two fields fell away gently towards the reed bed. To my right front there was a boundary belt, the other side of which comprised some rough land and fishing lakes. These lakes were fished day and night for carp and, although screened by trees from view, I was extremely wary about shooting in the direction of them. These self-imposed restrictions might seem to have been unduly limiting but I did not find this to be the case. It is true that sometimes I would spy a distant deer that came no nearer or disappeared altogether but, more often than not, it or another unseen beast would come my way.

I remember one early morning seeing two separate bucks at first light, both of which soon vanished. As the one I wanted to cull had been for a moment or two within range I was annoyed with myself for not having engaged him. As I tend to do after such moments of missed opportunity, I began the process of convincing myself that I would not see another buck all morning. I sat fidgeting in the Village High Seat, beating myself up for being so slow and for losing the opportunity. I opened and closed the numerous pockets of my deerstalking jacket, unzipping and zipping those with zip fastenings. I checked my ammunition pouch for the right number of rounds and my roe and predator calls. I applied my lens cloth to my binocular lenses and to the rifle scope and all the time I was painting myself into that place that bedevils novice deer stalkers namely "Chance Gone Corner".

In the hour that followed my state of mind prevented me from enjoying the fine early morning view and the miscellaneous animals and birds that were abroad. Time dragged and in so doing exaggerated my feelings of failure and hopelessness. I had reached the point of despair- the distinct view that this stalking game was not worth the candle- when both bucks appeared on the field again. After some false starts they both ran up the field towards me and then my cull buck turned and presented himself for a straightforward shot.

Defeat into victory! Despair into triumph! In a few seconds low ground deer stalking had once again become the best shooting pursuit in England. I dealt with the beast by the pond at the foot of the Village High Seat eventually hanging the eviscerated carcass on a convenient natural peg, a finger sized branch sawn off to a four inch length. I washed in the cold pond water and collected my kit. Then, in the increasing rays of the May morning sunshine I sat down at the base of a willow tree and luxuriated in it's warmth. After my early start, I dozed for a few minutes and, when I awoke, the birds and animals on the plain before me had all resumed their routines, which my shot had briefly disrupted. And so, shouldering my buck, I left that place as if I had never been there.

Chapter Seven

Peninsular Farm

WHILST ESTABLISHING MY deer management programme at Bourn Valley Farms, another local farmer asked me, and I use his words, "to knock over some of the deer" on his small farm. He had, I suppose, about 150 acres of arable land in the shape of a peninsular. His house and farm yard and a rectangular plantation were at what I would describe as the thick end and his fields tapered down in width at the far end to fifty yards or so. The distinctive feature of this flat, heavily walked land, and what I assume gave it it's name as a peninsular were the woods on either side of it. Inevitably the deer in these woods, which did not belong to my farmer client, came out to feed on his fields.

Although the farmer inferred that I could wander round with the expectation of shooting several of these greedy, visiting deer, I realised from the start that culling deer on Peninsular Farm was going to be nothing like as easy as that. There were several problems. First, the fields were very flat. Secondly, the tracks on it were heavily walked as were the paths and tracks within the adjoining woods. Thirdly, the farm backed on to a number of houses including the farm house which meant that some of the culling I would be attempting would take place just behind their back gardens. It was obvious to me that high seats were going to be essential, so I bought some more of these and had them delivered to the farm.

I erected the first of these in the far end of the rectangular spinney. Peninsular Wood was approximately 3 acres in extent, with predominantly mature Scots Pine and some under storey in the form of laurel, snowberry and cypress. A ditch ran through it. As is almost always the case, I had to undertake a good deal of lopping and pruning to create fields of view and fire but with some considerable amount of work succeeded in doing this. I arranged my seat so that when sitting in it I would be looking and shooting towards the far end of the farm, with my back to the farm yard, farm house and also the neighbouring houses. I also perfected my route into this high seat by clearing the ditch through the spinney and cutting some steps up the bank to enable me to access the high seat with the minimum of noise.

All this investment soon paid off as the venue was a most exciting one with deer to be seen more often than not. If they were not on the ground when I arrived, they would likely appear on the woodland edge and come in to feed. Some would feed on the fields but others would cross these and walk into Pensinular Wood itself more often than not underneath my high seat. On one of the first evenings I used this seat, two yearling roe bucks- brothers no doubt- appeared out of the adjoining wood and walked and ran over the field, which was then in stubble, towards my high seat. I took them both and remember driving on to the stubble and taking them both straight home to gralloch to avoid leaving traces of deer blood, pluck and paunch in the vicinity which might have discouraged other deer from visiting. Although I took this precaution, I soon formed the impression that the local deer learned very quickly that Peninsular Wood had become a dangerous location. Whilst not abandoning it completely, they became much more circumspect about using it. My success rate dropped off. One evening, as I surveyed the woodland boundary edge from my high seat, I spied a roe doe appear and stand quite still for many minutes. She could be seen minutely observing the farm fields between us. Eventually, she turned and disappeared in the woodland . I was puzzled by her vanishing act until I realised the direction of the breeze, and it was only a very slight one, had shifted and that she had caught my wind.

With the increasing caution of the deer coming on to Peninsular Farm, I decided to put up high seats nearer the boundaries of the farm with the adjoining woodland. One of these boundaries, immediately behind the houses, was formed by a hedge within which was a five acre field (my ground) and another hedge running away at right angles from it. The only place I could put a high seat was against an oak tree, which gave me a view of the five acre field immediately to my left and nearly the whole of Peninsular Farm in front and to my right. This high seat was really far too close to the hedge that separated the five acre field from the wood, being perhaps twenty yards from it at it's nearest point. However, this was the only place for it and I erected my high seat there really fearful that, because of it's proximity to the houses, it would be vandalised. I used quite a lot of camouflage netting to disguise it both from the deer and the public and am glad to say that many years later it is still there undamaged. Further, as the hedge has grown round it, the ladder and seat have become far less noticeable than they were in it's early years in this unusual location.

At that time, sound moderators were not allowed for full bore rifles and so every shot resulted in a loud report. I was all too well aware of this on the first early summer morning on which I used this high seat. It was, I recall, one of those calm summer mornings when you could hear a pin drop. I made it into the high seat without apparently spooking the deer, if any, that were nearby. In fact, I know I did because just a few minutes later a bold roe buck jumped out of the wood and prowled along the edge of the five acre field just my side of the hedge. He was on my ground and, under instructions from the farmer "not to take any prisoners", I had to engage him. It was awkward getting the rifle to my shoulder with him so close and before I could do so he had closed on me and come to an uneasy stop immediately in front of me. My shot, which was fatal for him, shattered the silence and was followed by a reverberating roar as it echoed off the wood side.

I have never sat so still as I did for the next few minutes, expecting windows to be flung open and doors to slam and the enraged and newly awakened population of the village to emerge as a lynch mob. I hunkered down in the high seat, hiding between the tree trunk at my back and the hedge and netting in front of me. I sat silently there and waited, with my roe buck lying on the field edge, all too visibly to my eyes. After a few minutes I realised no one was going to come out and remonstrate with me. In fact it seemed I had not awoken any one with my rifle shot. Descending cautiously, I swept my binoculars over the backs of the houses and saw no signs of activity and, in all cases drawn curtains. I had got away with it!

Emboldened by the lack of protests and interference I made much use of this seat both in the mornings and evenings. If my occasional shots, which always echoed spectacularly off the trees, kept their children awake the local parents never complained. I believe there was just one housewife who approached my farmer owner and attempted to persuade him to withdraw my permission on the grounds that my shooting disturbed her peace. As she at that time was the owner of a particularly persistently noisy and obnoxious terrier, a non-stop barker that kept all the neighbours permanently enraged, she got short shrift and was told to suck her orange.

I continued to cull from that high seat and one morning had an interesting experience. Approaching the seat very early, prior to the coming of a shooting light, I literally bumped into a roe buck which was on the point of emerging from the adjoining wood. He retreated, a little reluctantly I thought, barking persistently for some minutes from within the security of the woodland. Ordinarily, I would have retreated after such an encounter but for various reasons that was not an option there so I settled into the high seat and awaited developments. Sometime- perhaps half an hour - later and much to my surprise a roe buck, which I feel sure was the same one as I had disturbed earlier, came out, and I culled it. I learnt a lesson from this scenario, and thereafter did not always automatically abandon a stalk or sit up situation after such an encounter. Rather, if I felt the beast might be still close at hand and perhaps more puzzled than disturbed, I would gain confidence and wait in hiding with considerable confidence that it would show itself, just as this buck had done.

The two high seats I have described above lent themselves to use in north or east winds and this limited their availability as ours are prevailing south and south west winds. I therefore decided that I needed another high seat at the far end of Peninsular Farm, which would enable me to exploit the stalking there in these winds. I have mentioned above how at that far end of the farm the peninsular of land narrowed to a point and, to start with, I could not see how I could get in there without disturbing the deer. Rather against my better judgement, I took an ordinary aluminium ladder down to that end of the farm and left it at the bottom of an established oak tree that had a convenient fork in it twelve feet above the ground. A big branch of this had conveniently been removed some years previously, no doubt because it was overhanging the farmer's field. The remaining stump of this made a good, natural rest and, by sitting on an adjoining branch that was in tact, I could mount a long an effective watch over the edge of the neighbouring woodland.

As I relied here on emerging deer to come some way from their woodland sanctuary, this spot was best in the evening. From my natural vantage point I would usually pick up a party of roe deer plodding across the fields towards me. Often they would veer off and be lost to me but, sometimes they would come on and cross the middle ditch and into my killing zone, and this was exciting stuff. Mindful of my hard brief, I would then take a beast if there was one there in open season, and was to shoot several in this way.

There was one deer path leading into my ground at the very nose of the peninsular and, now and then, a deer or two would come in unseen by me. The first I knew of them was when they appeared, as if by magic, slightly front right of my perch. I can recall quite clearly an old roe buck appearing before me in this way and how he picked his unhurried way along the brew of the ditch, moving from left to right. I remember how he covered a lot of ground in spite of his stops and starts. He was oblivious of the imminent danger he was in and, I think, to the bullet that dispatched him. There was a stream of sorts there, at that end of the farm and, as I had a long carry, I gralloched him there and washed myself and my knife in the clear running water. When next I visited that place, only a day or two later, all the pluck had been eaten by foxes or badgers.

I have, so far, recounted my culling of one or two roe bucks on Peninsular Farm but this only covers a small part of my involvement there. I was then or later also to be involved in culling other deer – roe deer does, muntjac and fallow- and I will refer to these culls in due course as they were to provide me with much fascinating deerstalking and interesting incidents. As this was the case with almost all my deer stalking grounds, I shall refer to some of these later. I certainly would wish to disabuse anyone who had the impression that my low ground stalking has comprised a few summer outings after roe bucks. Although roe buck stalking has provided me with some of the most thrilling low ground deerstalking experiences, it has only formed a small part of my whole culling activity, with much more time being put in at roe and fallow does and at muntjac bucks and does.

Chapter Eight

A Deerstalking Partnership

I HAVE RELATED HOW at first I made my own way as a low ground deerstalker, and how I developed my own deerstalking and deer management techniques at Bourn Valley Farms and at Peninsular Farm. Although I was quite happy to run my own deerstalking from the start, I made and retained a good friend at that time, who helped me a lot. His name was BallisticTip."Tip", as his many friends and connections know him, was a professional soldier, an infantryman who served in Germany after the end of the Second World War. He did not waste his time there. Having had an interest in field sports since his boyhood, he found there the true passion of his sporting life namely low ground deer stalking. Whilst in Germany with the British Army of Occupation, Tip studied and learnt German deer management, and so was one of the several servicemen who brought these enlightened methods back to the U.K.

Tip was and is an expert rifle shot who has continued to hone his rifle shooting skills throughout his deerstalking career. Living in Colchester, within rifle range of it's Middlewick and Fringinghoe Ranges he has probably fired more rounds down the butts there than any other man alive. The first lesson I learned from him as a rifleman was that it was impossible to practice too much. Tip's skill and dedication were not to be faulted. His second lesson in this department was over the care of equipment. By the time I knew him he was a most methodical rifleman but, perhaps, he had always been that. However, I can recall watching him shoot home loaded cartridges with three or four different calibre rifles on the range and record orderly data as to the accuracy of these throughout a whole shoot, pausing only to advise or assist tyros such as myself. His was a model of self discipline and good personal organisation on the firing point.

Tip invited me to shoot on the Ranges and for a year or two I often drove over to Colchester for these shoots. I learnt something of rifle shooting by practising but a lot more through his advice and instruction. I certainly put some rounds through my first deer calibre rifles on those Ranges. The advantage of shooting on the Ranges was that one could shoot safely in an unhurried and unconcerned manner. The disadvantage was the time it took and the expense of it with fuel, ammunition and range fees all to be taken into account, particularly when one was travelling a long distance to and from the Ranges.

Having stalking rights over a variety of different farms, I originally thought I would find several places where I could have my own range and shoot a big rifle regularly. Surprisingly this was not so and possible locations often had to be ruled out because of the proximity of houses, farm buildings, roads or footpaths. Not infrequently I found, and still find now, that I have to restrict my "checking zero" sessions to two or three hurried shots to get done whilst I know a location is clear. That said, once a sporting rifle is sighted in, regular checks to ensure it is holding zero are all that is usually needed to maintain it's accuracy and thereby the confidence of the rifleman using it.

By way of reciprocation, I invited Tip to stalk with me during the roe rut on Bourn Valley Farms. I well remember the morning he came as I took him to the Village High Seat described previously. He arrived in good time, in the pre- dawn dark and I guided him into the High Seat without, so far as I knew, disturbing any deer in it's locality. We both climbed up into the High Seat and I perched rather uncomfortably on a branch whilst Tip, as my guest rifle for the morning, sat in the seat and prepared himself for action. That rut, there were fields of standing wheat either side of the grass field in front of the Village High Seat. This restricted the view to the grass field unless a deer was to put it's head up or jump and chase in the ripe corn.

I was very confident that I would be able to show Tip some deer as I had been watching them from this high seat. I had, in particular, watched two bucks that appeared to live in the area. The first was a particularly fine looking young buck with a beautiful head for the three or four year old I estimated him to be. He really had something about him and I had christened him "the Dandy". His arch enemy was the other buck that occupied that territory: the Rottweiler. He, in contrast, was a sour looking bruiser of a deer which I saw constantly patrolling the boundaries of the grass field. His head was poor but such was his obvious strength that I feared for the Dandy. I resolved to cull the Rottweiler.

I had explained this plan to Tip so that he was briefed as to the buck I wanted shot.

"How will I know which is the Rottweiler?" he enquired in a whisper.

"You'll know when you see the brute" I quietly replied.

The light came soon enough, as it always does in late July, and before very long the Rottweiler jumped into the field from the standing wheat and made off down the field on one of his typical patrols. He was within range when he first appeared but gone before Tip could engage him. We waited in the Village High Seat overlooking an empty field until, in the distance down the hill I thought I saw more than one deer move, although I couldn't be sure. As a novice deerstalker and host for the morning, I was becoming rather nervous as nothing was happening and I wished very much for Tip to have a shot.

Then, as so often seems to happen in low ground stalking, our luck changed. There was some flurry of activity on the right hand side of the field, and then the Rottweiler was returning. He came up the edge of the field towards us until he reached a round thorn tree about eighty yards in front of us. Here he slowed up, stopped, turned and fell as Tip, with the minimum of fuss and movement, shot him in the bottom half of his heart. Tip gralloched him at the foot of the High Seat and I remember that too as he did the job with neat, economical movements and an extremely sharp knife.

That was a happy morning and one to be long remembered. Years later, I was tickled to be introduced by Tip as "David, who had allowed him (Tip) to shoot one of his special bucks." Well, in a way he was right. The Rottweiler was a brute, a bruiser, a bully: a special buck.

Tip did not have a great deal of roe deerstalking so when I was offered the stalking rights over a farm not far from there, I accepted them and invited him to join me as my deer stalking partner on Maytree Farm. The land concerned was typical of Suffolk and Essex, being flattish arable farm land with a couple of ancient woodlands, and some adjoining forestry that did not form part of the land over which I had permission to stalk.

We invested in some high seats and put these up in strategic places. After a couple of years we approached one or two neighbours and added to our holding. We saw a few deer- almost all roe- and a certain amount of deer sign. Our brief from the landowner was one of exercising reasonable control rather than attempting elimination and, over many years, we have enjoyed interesting but not spectacular deer stalking there.

As this venture was an informal partnership, I drew up and agreed rules of engagement with Tip so we both knew where we stood . He, being retired, was to stalk during the week whilst I had first call at week-ends. I stipulated that no guests be allowed to protect Tip from the plethora of would be stalkers without their own stalking, who used to plague him to take them out. I wanted this to be a place for him, particularly as I was very busy working at that time and had little time for regular culling there.

I think it is true to say that for many years Tip derived a great deal of satisfaction from this little roe deer management assignment. For years, whilst I was practising law full time, he shot most of the deer and I was quite happy with that, having taken on the stalking primarily for his benefit and enjoyment. And no one enjoyed deer stalking more than Tip. Now and then we would stalk together and that was fun too. On other occasions, when I was too busy to do my own reconnaissance, Tip would call me and say something like "… *if you walk past the pond area which was coppiced last year and wait in the temporary high seat by the hedge end, then you should get a shot at the old five point buck.*" Invariably, I did.

The roe deer on and about Maytree Farm had an interesting way of altering their behaviour between winter and summer. In the summer months they favoured the woods and hedgerows and, here and there, it would be possible to find a doe and kids or a buck and doe enjoying life as a discreet family unit. These animals were well protected from view in the summer months by the wall to wall crops of cereals grown on the farm. Only the deer stalker, out at the earliest hour, would be likely to encounter summer deer if they came out to graze on the mown grass paths or, perhaps, on a field of young sugar beet seedlings.

One early summer morning I accounted for a nice young cull roe buck by exploiting this. There was a long, narrow meadow on the farm with a public road at the south end and a game crop comprising artichokes at the other, with a plantation of young trees and bushes offset to the East of this. A public footpath ran along the west side of the game cover and the meadow and this was mown short to facilitate walking. The whole area was very flat and it was impracticable if not downright unsafe to shoot from the ground. However, three quarters of the way along the meadow, and overlooking the game cover, was a good high heap of straw and horse muck, which were no doubt the remainings from the stables of the farmer's wife. Having one morning seen two bucks in this meadow, I decided to return and try for them. From the road, I used a screen of thorns to get to the west side of the meadow. I glassed all round to check for deer, but could not see any. I then dropped into the deep ditch that separated the meadow from the footpath and made my way along the bottom of it. Now and then, I was obstructed by brambles and these I pruned with my pocket secateurs so that I could pass noiselessly.

My next problem was caused by a tree stump that had fallen into the ditch and around which a good deal of bramble, sweethearts, thistles and other rubbish had grown unmolested by the flail. There was too much of this to snip so I had to get out of the ditch and crawl round the place before dropping back in again. I did not encounter any deer during this part of my manoeuvre. I kept to the ditch just once pulling myself up so that I could look round, just to make sure I was not bumping any deer that might be out there. At long last, I reached a stoway, a few yards beyond which was the muck heap, which was my intended observation and firing point. There was nothing for it but to crawl through the stinging nettles and wet grass and then to clamber up the back of the heap. This last part looked easy enough from the bottom but, when I came to do it, I found it hard to attain a grip on the friable, damp surface of the heap and had to struggle a bit to achieve a position that enabled me to view the foreground, and, if necessary, engage a buck.

What I saw, as I settled down, confirmed that my elaborately discreet access arrangements had been very necessary. There were deer there in front of me, not in the game crop or the plantation but in a length of thick hedge the other side of the cover. Their activities there showed they were undisturbed and I watched them for some time with the fascination I always derive from watching roe deer in their own world. Then their movements ceased and they were gone, not quickly or running away but by melting into the undergrowth.

It was some time before I saw so much as an ear again and, when I did, it was of two deer quite far out in a hedge running away to the west. Whether these were the ones I had been watching or different ones I could not say. Whether there was a buck there I could not see. And then, suddenly, there was a buck, a young cull buck, making towards me along the footpath. There I was, lying on the back elevation of the heap, rifle resting on my day sack, with a clear view of the game cover in front of me and the footpath at 11 o'clock with a good, safe background view behind it. There was a point, at about forty yards, at which I could shoot but I realised that if the buck came on I should never be able to turn to my left and take a shot. The buck had to be stopped and I selected the stopping point by reference to a convenient ragwort plant. As the roe buck reached it, I called out "Halt!" and he paused, less afraid than uneasy, giving me time enough to do what I had to do.

Before I carried him out, I washed his blood off the grass on the footpath. In another couple of hours the usual woman in the blue shell suit would jog down the footpath and, with a little care and a lot of water, I ensured she would never know what had gone on there earlier that May morning.

In the winter, I would have expected these roe deer to retreat to the warmth and shelter of the woods and to restrict their movement as far as they could to the immediate vicinity of their couching areas, particularly in bad weather. However, for some reason- the woods being driven regularly for game shooting perhaps- many of these roe formed small herds and took up winter residence in the largest fields on the farm, often annexing the grassy base of the apex formed by electricity pylons as the centre of their territory. So long as they stayed there they were safe! These winter roe have often had the last laugh on us as, after a blank morning in the high seats, we have had to watch them feeding four or five hundred yards away in the middle of a flat field surrounded by roads and houses. These were smart deer that were unapproachable, unsafe and immune against lead poisoning and, worse still, highly visible to the farmer owner of Maytree Farm.

I have read that roe deer in Eastern Europe are prone to herd during the cold winter months and no doubt they profit from the benefits derived from being in the herd such as the provision of mutual warmth and shelter and as a defence against predators. I have experienced it in a small way on my stalking grounds in Suffolk where I have at various times seen groups of seven and eleven. Once, and only once, on land adjoining Maytree Farm, I saw a herd of seventeen roe deer and this is the most I have ever seen together at one time. That herd was, it seemed, led by the biggest roe buck I have ever seen. Although I looked out for him many times after that sighting, I never saw him again. He was so big, both in bodyweight and head, that sometimes I wonder whether I ever saw him at all.

In case I have given the impression that the deer at Maytree Farm all and always relied on distance to keep safe, I can give several examples of contrary behaviour. One such anecdote was related to me by the farmer owner. He told me he had been walking round the perimeter hedge and ditch of one of his fields when he spotted a roe deer curled asleep up in a hollow tree stump. He was, he said, a yard from it. On another occasion, in high summer, I had a long fruitless walk and stalk outing which, combined with a very early pre-dawn start, made me feel tired. When the sun came up, and it became pleasantly warm, I made myself comfortable in a sunny spot at the corner of one of the woods. I had at that time a wild black Labrador dog named Luke. On this occasion even Luke was ready for a rest so I didn't feel guilty at all by taking time out for a lie-down. I have no idea how long we were there as I soon fell asleep. I do know that I was woken up by Luke (on his lead) dancing a desperate jig on my recumbent body as he tried to get loose and chase a really fine roe buck that was standing twenty yards away watching us. Completely sky lined, with the farmhouse and buildings behind him, he was as safe as he would have been in the middle of one of my large fields.

Over the years we had good times at Maytree Farm, but we also had our troubles there too. We had a high seat stolen by one of the local residents, who was inherently and irrationally hostile to our activities. Fortunately, he moved away. Over the years, we had a number of amateur or part time gamekeepers working on the ground. Some were proper people; others didn't respect either the deer or our deerstalking rights. The most blatant of these requested us to support his firearms application for a deer calibre rifle. He assured us that were it granted and he purchased such a weapon he would not deploy it against our deer. As he was the worst culprit for shooting deer locally with unlawful calibre rifles, his request was given short shrift. Finally, on the negative side, I should mention the large number of ramblers who used the roads and footpaths around Maytree Farm. The high volume of this human traffic and the large number of routes severely limited safe, effective stalking times. I know this is a problem everywhere, but at Maytree Farm it was particularly acute. Usually, at least the first couple of hours of a long light summer morning would be rambler free, but in winter, with light not coming before seven we came to expect that our first sighting of the morning would be human rather than cervid. After some years of this we discontinued our doe culling there in early December and returned again, with the longer mornings in February, hoping we could catch up then and cull our target numbers. More often than not we made it.

Whilst I would not wish all my stalking situations to be conducted with a partner I greatly enjoyed the partnership I had with Tip. First, enabling him to partake in some reasonable roe deer stalking free of the hassle and politics of club stalking pleased me. Secondly, it was satisfying for us together to do a good job and maintain, as we did, a reasonable balanced population of healthy deer. Third, and I am unabashed in saying it in these precise words, it was great fun.

Chapter Nine

Estate Deer Management

I HAVE RECOUNTED HOW I soon became involved in the management and stalking of farm deer. I was lucky in this as, in the case of each farm I took on the issues were simple and similar. It was straightforward to organise the cull of up to half a dozen roe deer and to assess and split this cull between bucks and does and by age range. It gave me the chance to understand the politics of farm life. Then and now there may be very few persons employed on arable farms, but many are involved in them. This meant that, at times, my paths would cross those of not only the farmer owner and his family but farm managers, agronomists, contractors, casual workers, foresters, game keepers, shoot lessees, ministry folk, ornithologists, beekeepers and many others. As the deer manager, I found I sometimes needed to keep at least some of these involved or at least aware of what I was doing. I soon found I could not be an entirely separate, isolated operator without reference to anyone or anything else.

This proved to be good preparation for the next assignment that came my way. This was an invitation to take over the deer management of the Eden Vale Estate, which I shall here call "Eve" for short. In deer management terms, this was a greater challenge.

The Estate comprised three thousand five hundred acres of land in Suffolk on what had once been several smaller farms. Unusually, this was quite different in character. One end had heavy, clod sticky clay. This was the land I had grown up with and, at it's most sticky it really inhibits getting about on foot let alone actually stalking deer on it. The difficulty of working such soil in the winter also affects the farming of it, as agricultural operations on and over these heavy land farms largely cease between November and March. The light land, at the other end of the farm, was over chalk and was and is largely down land with big fields and some pleasing contour in places. Here, on a summer day, one might imagine oneself to be on a small corner of the Hampshire downs.

Both the light and heavy land farms had a number of woods on them. The woods on the light land were mainly belts and small woods originally planted for game shooting. These had a good mix of tree species and, in places, interesting drifts of under storey cover such as box, lonicera and snowberry. The beech belts, which had long been an attractive feature in one area, were, at that time, in the process of being replanted in the aftermath of the 1987 gale in which many of the mature beeches had been destroyed.

The heavy land woods were for the most part examples of ancient wet woodland. Mainly but not entirely hardwoods, with a great deal of oak and ash, there were also compartments of conifers and hazel coppice. The heavy land woods were bigger and quite different in character to those on the light land.

At that time the forestry contractors were busy on the light land replanting the lost beeches , but were also working to a plan in the heavy land woods in which they were undertaking a considerable amount of coppicing.

The owners took a close and active interest in the forestry programme and, when I first looked round, I was impressed by the high standard of the woodland management and awed by such well kept woods. I had since nothing so impressive, so obviously well loved and cared for since, as a small boy, I had walked through his estate woods with RAV.

All the farming was in hand and was carried on by a farm manager and his team. There was also a gamekeeper who was mainly focused on the light land end of the Estate, as it was there that the best and most sporting game shooting was to be had, and also there that he released most of his reared pheasants. The Estate was not shot over more than half a dozen days a year and these were modest, family days.

As might be expected there was a good deal of game on the Estate and the sight of this, when I first looked round further demonstrated to me that this was a properly run place. I was still more impressed to see a few roe deer close to a track I was on and to have the keeper tell me that they were always there or thereabouts. They must have been quite unmolested to become so tame.

There were other deer, mainly roe and muntjac on the light land and roe, muntjac and fallow in and about the heavy land woods. It was obvious that in places there were large populations of muntjac and fallow, although no one knew how large. This state of affairs was caused at least in part by the absence of any deer culling for the previous two years after the owners had had a bad experience with the previous deer manager, who had gone. Another factor was the immigration of fallow deer from what was in effect an unfenced deer sanctuary adjacent to one side of the heavy land. This land comprised one hundred and fifty acres of derelict mixed woodland and paddocks and was unshot for either deer or small game. The owners of the sanctuary were not shooting people and, apparently loved the deer. The fallow in this sanctuary could literally step though the hedge when they wanted to enter the Estate's land, which they did because the supply of feed in the sanctuary was wholly inadequate to support the large numbers of them that lived in it.

It should be clear from the thumbnail sketch above that Eve was a serious agricultural estate operated on a proper stewardship basis. My brief, if I accepted it, was to reduce and control the deer populations for the protection of plantings, coppice, growing timber and crops. I was to do this as best I could in season and in daylight, and generally in accordance with the law. I was not to shoot any trophy bucks. Although I was welcome to call on my friends for assistance with culling I was not to charge anyone for an outing. This second rule was to save me from coming under pressure to shoot or allow to be shot the beasts with the best heads.

I could readily recognise the amount of work that would be required of a Deer Manager at Eve. If I was going to do it, I was determined to do it properly but, at that time, I was busy and had a burgeoning law practice many miles away. I was apprehensive as to whether I could do the job and whether I should, having regard to the amount of time I should have to commit to it. In the end I was so impressed by the owners and their team that I agreed to accept the assignment and, in so doing, set a life course by which, many years later, I am still happily steering. Inevitably, many of the experiences and incidents recorded in the rest of this book flow from my tenure as the Deer Manager of Eve, and from the paths of the deer that I have followed there down all these years.

I started my assignment by walking and reporting. I found there to be deer all over the heavy land and in most places on the light land. I ordered a dozen high seats as there were none there. I still have them, much repainted and repaired and many deer have been shot from some of them. I needed a deer larder, and a cool room, formerly used exclusively as a game larder, was adapted and had a rail and pulley system installed to my design to facilitate the handling and storage of carcasses. Later on, a quad bike for the extraction of carcasses was acquired, which brought to an end a lot of time consuming, back breaking work with the drag rope. More recently, a chiller was also installed which has alleviated the danger of losing carcasses to flies or decomposition in warm weather.

As the deer larder and chiller, washing facilities and quad bike garage were all situated in the owners' back yard, and as they walked and rode in the same woods as I would be stalking in, it was obvious I would not be able to operate invisibly. I therefore needed to give notice of when I was planning to stalk to enable the owners and anyone else, such as the gamekeeper, who needed to know to be brought into the loop. I devised a simple form of single page notice which enabled me to give notice of my intention of stalking, and who, if anyone, would accompany me. I included one section in this for recording how many and what species of deer I had seen and shot, and a comments section which enabled me to retail any other interesting incidents, such as a view of a fox or badger or, perhaps, a suspicious vehicle or individual. I simply faxed these notices the day or evening before visiting Eve for stalking purposes. This ensured the owners knew when I was coming and enabled them to put me on notice if my visit was likely to conflict with another activity on the Estate such as a farm walk or a visit from the Hunt. The simple data recorded also enabled me to double check my cull records and helped ensure that all beasts culled got into the end of season report.

We convened one meeting a year, usually in March (the end of the open season for does then falling at the end of February), at which I presented the cull figures achieved and agreed cull targets for the following year. Although this involved a certain amount of desk work, it was worthwhile. Our meetings were always interesting and enabled all of us involved to build and maintain understanding of each other's points of view and to tackle the challenges of deer management on Eve.

The development of my role as a deer manager and the annual cull at Eve involved me in many more facets than in my much more limited local culls and my experiences as a solicitor were probably of more help to me in this than my skills as a low ground deerstalker. Over many years, I like to think I gradually grew into the deer manager's role and became comfortable with it. However, never knowing when it might end, and hugely enjoying my roe deer stalking at home, I retained and still retain my local deer stalking where I can prowl about happily in pursuit of the occasional roe and muntjac deer.

One of the immediate benefits of taking over the deer management at Eve was that it hugely increased the scope of my deerstalking activities. For instance, it gave me much more scope for calling both roe and muntjac deer.

By then I was, I thought, a reasonably accomplished roe deer caller. Using a variety of wood and plastic calls, calls with a reed for preference, I had some thrilling experiences. I culled my first buck – a young roe with a light four point head – from just inside the edge of a thicket. He came in very close and I succeeded in threading my shot through an assortment of young whips and shoots.

On another morning, I called a roe buck through a field of standing wheat. A big buck he came at the gallop until I held him up on the grass in front of my high seat.

Eve's Cattle Grove Wood was home to the best buck on the Estate for several years and once a year, in the rut, I would call him up for inspection. He had a medal head and lived to a ripe old age.

One August evening, during the roe rut, I visited a square wood of six acres where I had seen several roe deer. I knew there were two roe deer resident in or at least in the vicinity of this wood. I planned in advance to shoot the smaller of the two, in the hope that the fraying would be reduced. There was no natural position from which to call in this wood as the under storey was so thick. Eventually I sat down on a bank at the edge of the wood which allowed me no more than twenty five yards visibility. I started calling and very soon a roe buck responded by partially emerging from the thicket in front of me. I dispatched him. Going to look at him, I realised at once he was the big buck and not the yearling for which I had taken him. It was too late to put that right by then so I started to gralloch that buck in the wood, in a clearing in the coppice. A few minutes into this a young tree began to shake, as if in the wind, and it took me a few moments to remember it was a calm afternoon, Picking up the rifle I tried a few more squeaks from where I stood which to my amazement produced the yearling buck. Such was the desirability of roe deer for that wood, at that stage, there was another buck in situ within a week.

Once in Argyllshire, a red deer stalker took me out in the low ground around the policies of the main house. There was there, she told me, a roe buck with a strange antler. She said she had little knowledge of roe deer but that there was something odd about this one on one side of the head. Starting to call, as we stood well concealed in some bracken, this buck appeared once in the open and, seconds later, at my knee before withdrawing a few yards which enabled me to shoot him. I marvelled at the atrophied right hand rack – a scallop shaped coronet with several short spikes sticking out of it. All the stalker said was "He came so close I thought you would stick him!"

I found that the roe calling process was simply not as certain as it looked. One morning after calling from the edge of a field of standing wheat without success, I went to sleep in the field margin and awoke thirty minutes later to find a roe buck very cautiously approaching. He had delayed a long time before answering the call.

On another afternoon, I called from the corner of a wood and, on giving up rather too soon, I walked clear of the wood and met a roe buck coming along the outside of it, where the going was easier.

Once, calling from the ground with my son in a high seat, it was sometime before the buck disentangled himself from my vicinity to present him with a clear, safe shot.

I realise roe deer calling can be criticised for taking advantage of the buck during the rut and for highlighting the roe buck rather than the doe for culling. However, there is no need to shoot a specific roe buck just because it comes to the call. From the outset I was choosy as to which buck I shot. Similarly, with muntjac calling. There is no need to shoot a muntjac doe which has, or appears likely to have, a fawn at heel. Both roe and muntjac may be called, inspected and, if the stalker desires, spared. Unless the landowner insists they be shot, there is no obligation on the deerstalker to shoot any particular deer.

My involvement with Eve gave full scope to my aspirations in deer management and to the practical aspects of culling deer by all legal means available to me. Calling roe and muntjac deer were to become important "tools" in achieving this task.

Chapter Ten

Fallow Bucks and Prickets

I N MY FIRST autumn's stalking season at Eve I soon became aware that there were significant numbers of big fallow bucks there on the heavy land. I heard groaning in most of the woods and saw fresh scrapes in the rides. I saw some fallow bucks with impressive antlers. As I very little experience of fallow deer I invited an expert over to stalk and to give me an opinion on the quality of the bucks on Eve. He was an experienced fallow deerstalker, having had the management of land and woods heavily invested in them in other parts of the country.

His morning visit was fortunately productive and he shot a muntjac. More fortunately still, he saw a couple of fallow bucks close up and was ecstatic about their quality. He admired their appearance, obviously heavy body weight and their massive palmate antlers. He confirmed my uninformed belief that these were wild fallow bucks of the highest possible quality. These were deer so magnificent that they made me and every one of my deerstalking guests gasp when we saw them. I then saw the wisdom of owners' blanket prohibition on shooting trophy bucks on Eve. I had no desire to shoot one and the occasional guests with aspirations to do so were emphatically instructed to shoot nothing bigger than sorrels. No one has ever breached this rule and the quality of the best fallow bucks on Eve remains very high, even though, for external reasons outside my control, they are not so numerous as they were when I first saw them.

Going back to that first season, I remember starting my fallow cull in the rut. Using high seats in the woods which hosted rutting stands, I picked off odd prickets that were hanging about hoping for some action. I had some exciting times waiting in my seat for the light to come, listening to the stand buck groaning, and hearing the uncharacteristic noise of fallow deer moving over the woodland floor incautiously and often at speed. The first of the prickets that I shot walked through the trees and stopped between myself and the stand buck. I couldn't see the stand buck but I could see quite clearly that the pricket was either watching him or the activities going on around him. The pricket, a common with a light coloured coat, was intently observing the scene down the hill .After a little time he turned and presented for a shot which I took. A few moments later, I saw a parcel of does fading away through the trees but the big buck didn't stop groaning and the action on the rutting stand continued until I went in with the rope to drag out my beast. At that point, I could have easily dispatched the master buck but, as I was to very soon learn, fallow does are the difficult deer to stalk. In comparison, the bucks are really easy.

Another discovery I made that morning was that male fallow deer are horrible to handle during the rut. Even my pricket, although hardly old enough to be the Romeo of the wood, was a leaking, stinking ,sweating, dirty brute. His rank smell soon transferred itself to my clothes, car and every other object with which the carcass came into contact. Later in the same rut, I shot a sorrel that was even smellier than the pricket had been. Having no aspirations to take any trophy heads at all, I began to question whether I wanted to be culling the majority of the male fallow deer in my cull plan during the rut at all. It seemed to be an unsatisfactory time to be accounting for them when they were so smelly and dirty and probably far from palatable on the table.

Once again it was an old hand who pointed me in the right direction. He advised me to start shooting prickets right from the beginning of their long open season in August. This hint caused me to start watching my fallow deer more closely than I had been at that time of year (probably because I had formerly been exclusively preoccupied with the roe deer rut). Once I started to watch fallow deer in August I observed the propensity of the prickets to emerge from the woods and prowl the fields, driven by an apparently irresistible urge to go walk-about. Sitting in some good vantage point, and sweeping the hedgerows with my binoculars would quite often result in my spying a pair of prickets taking the fresh air. These would be quite discreet, half hidden by standing crop and tall hedgerows.

I set up a number of high seats to help me get on terms with these wanderers. The Sunset High Seat soon became one of my favourites. Positioned on a tree in a boundary hedge, it faced back into a field belonging to Eve. Eighty yards to it's left was a wood that formed part of the sanctuary I have referred to previously. Sitting in the high seat, Eve's field was in front of the stalker, and the boundary to the left was formed by this woodland edge. There was a field behind the seat which did not belong to Eve. In certain wind directions that field was more favoured by fallow deer than was the Eve field, but there was nothing I could do about that except be sure to use my Sunset seat as often as possible in a west or north westerly winds, both of which caused the field close to the wood to be sheltered and extremely deer friendly.

On my first visit to Sunset, I waited until I thought it too dark to shoot before descending from the seat. I am not sure whether I had actually got to the bottom of the ladder before the deer emerged from the wood or if the two events were simultaneous. Whichever it was, there was a stand-off for a few moments with the fallow uncertain as to what they were seeing whilst sure they were seeing something. I was definitely not intending to discharge a shot that would, from where I stood on the ground, have likely passed through a deer and continued into the woodland. The matter was resolved by the lead doe in the parcel of fallow deciding all was not well and rushing back into the woodland with a bark of alarm. I noticed that a large, pale pricket in the group was the last to leave and only abandoned his evening's intended grazing with reluctance. From the foot of the high seat I disconsolately observed his departure but thought that I would recognise him if I saw him again.

On my next visit, a couple of days later, I was by chance rather earlier in arriving and settled myself comfortably in Sunset, which was bathed in the late afternoon sun. I had a flask of tea with me and poured myself a drink of it into the cap. I then sat there preoccupied with my own thoughts. I had little expectation of seeing any deer until the sun had set and the light deteriorated. I just sat still and enjoyed the late summer afternoon sunshine and such birds as I could see. And then, quite suddenly, a large pale coloured pricket appeared out of the wood to the forward left of me, and started to stroll down the edge in my direction. After walking for some distance, he turned across my front, speeding up to cross the open stubble in my foreground. I thought I recognised him, tracking him with my rifle rested on the roll of grey foam round the shooting rail. "Hi there!" I called and he paused long enough for the 130 grain bullet to take him in the top of the heart. A last hopeless lunge and his life was gone. My first August pricket was down in the field, and when I walked over to inspect him I admired this young animal, which was in prime summer condition.

Later, in the deer larder, he weighed ninety pounds as a cleaned carcass still in his skin but with his head and legs off. Inspecting the large amount of fat on him and his fine condition confirmed to me that culling fallow prickets in August and September before the rut should become a culling priority, and it did. At that time, I was uncertain as to whether enough prickets could be culled to make the effort involved worthwhile but, quite soon, outings like the one described above, were rewarded, not every time of course, but sufficiently often to make me persist in them.

If I could get out on a hot, sultry August afternoon and evening, I would be very confident of catching out a pricket. Putting myself into a pricket's skin so to speak I realised how he would find the conifer wood stale and airless and how the flies would bite him. I could imagine his longing for a wander along the ditches and hedgerows in the arable land becoming irresistible. I guessed he would approach and then stand for a long time just within the woodland edge studying the scene outside for movement, danger and people. Then he would commit and, just as I had seen him do it, emerge to stand and stroll on the stubble field or crop and to wander in the fresh air with here and there a trace of clean refreshing breeze.

The next pricket I shot from the Sunset seat came from my right. I picked up him and his mate through the binoculars when they were still five hundred yards away and swivelled round in the seat to observe them the better. There was a common coloured pricket, which looked quite small beside his sturdy, dark coated companion. When they got closer I could see the black beast was a flat top. He had no spikes at all; just two egg shaped, egg sized knobs. He was big, no doubt because all his energy had gone into growing body weight; none into growing racks. The two wanderers came along the hedgerow, along the Eve side of it on the same route as I had walked in an hour before. They were on my ground and would be safe to shoot, but would they come on? They could readily walk through a gap in the straggly hedge and be over the boundary in a stride. They could just as easily pass behind – out of bounds- as in front. They kept coming, in shot now but awkward, heads on to me, and restless with it. The smaller animal was in front.

Then I had one of those breaks the low ground stalker needs now and then. It came from the sky in the form of a small helicopter flying over the land behind me at low level – perhaps a flying taxi delivering a jockey to Newmarket. Whatever it was, it caused a tremor of alarm in my quarry. They did not spook seriously but moved out into the field away from the noise and made to pass in front of me. This necessitated my moving the rifle from the side to the front rail of the seat to take a lean for a shot at twelve o'clock. My luck held as the dark beast obligingly stopped and presented a straight forward shot. There was no chance of a shot at the common pricket, which ran into the wood unsaluted, leaving his mate dead on the field.

Another pricket from this productive seat kept me waiting until the last possible moment for a shot. I had sat up for what seemed like hours without seeing so much as a deer's ear and, whilst not bored, I was despondent. I wanted to pack up as the gloaming intensified but mindful of my previous late evening encounter, I stayed where I was. I kept sweeping the woodland edge to my left with my binoculars and, on what I resolved would be my very last sweep, I saw a pale shape just inside the wood where I was sure there had not been any pale shape before. I watched and waited and then the shape moved, disappeared for a moment and re-appeared on the field with others pouring out behind it. It was easier to see now against the yellow straw of the wheat stubble. The pale beast was a fallow doe. The rest of them were does and calves. It was too dark to sex the calves. I could see a dozen or so does and followers... surely, I thought, there must be a pricket. Then there was one and I engaged him without delay. Chaos ensued with deer running in all directions completely confused by the report of the echoing off the wood side.

Temporarily blinded by the flash of the rifle's muzzle and the recoil, I looked for my beast on the stubble. I couldn't see him. I came down from the high seat with mounting anxiety. I was worried by not being able to see my beast down and went forward concerned he had run off wounded into the trees. I went to the spot where I thought he had been standing, but when I got there it looked different in the dark and from ground level. I had a head torch, which I wore on my forehead and looked for blood from the beast, but couldn't see any sign. I began to feel remorse for taking the shot so late in so little light. Going forward I shone the beam of the small torch in the ditch on the woodland edge. Nothing! Nothing at all! I felt the deepest gloom; a growing, awful sense of desolation. I went out into the stubble and looked again thinking that I might find some sign but did not. Then I circled round and returned to the ditch a few yards further up than I had the last time. The thin beam travelled along the ditch and, yes, there he was. He had never made it over the ditch and lay head under legs were he had tumbled in his death flight.

My sombre mood was at once displaced by elation. I was delighted, happy, successful and satisfied. I had outwaited and outwitted another pricket. I am ashamed to say my previous thoughts about the inadvisability of taking so late a shot were quite extinguished by my sense of triumph. Such, I fear, is the deerstalker's psyche.

I felt no compunction about stalking my boundary with the sanctuary land and woods as no deer control was undertaken there and a burgeoning population was doing untold damage on Eve. Much of this damage was caused by the deer visiting Eve during the night, which they could readily do by popping across the ditch dividing the two estates.

The preferred route of the fallow was in the top corner of the boundary field belonging to Eve, this being the shortest point between the north corner of the sanctuary woodland and the south side of Eve's Twenty Wood. After studying the topography of this field very closely, I decide to make use of the ditch between the two estates for ambush purposes. This involved me in making a long approach either in the pre dawn darkness on a morning outing or in the late afternoon before an evening session. As there would often be fallow out grazing on the sanctuary grassland, this was a critical although not immediately productive part of the plan.

In the evening, I would hide in the ditch with my rifle ready for use in front of me when and if fallow jumped into Eve's field over, as it were, my right shoulder. As I did not have permission to shoot on the sanctuary, I had to carry on with the spectre of fallow deer breathing down my neck or kicking me as they jumped the ditch at last light and then had to wait until they worked round into the safe killing zone in front of me.

In fact, the mornings gave better sport as the shot, if I was lucky enough to get one, would be at deer crossing the field in front of me, walking or running towards me in their haste to retreat to the safety of the sanctuary. Inevitable, with the flank being a wide one, some beasts would by-pass me without having an inkling of how lucky they were. These beasts would be in my sight all the way from Eve's woodland edge, over the field, and until they slipped back into the sanctuary and made their way over it's paddocks behind me.

One crisp September morning I lay in wait and spotted a parcel of fallow does with a sorrel in the rear emerge from a small belt beyond Twenty Wood. I expected this party to pass five hundred yards to my right and leave my ground without offering me a shot. For whatever reason, perhaps sheer exuberance on such a beautiful morning, they all ran towards me. I had a bipod fitted to my rifle and lay on the brew of the bank tracking these deer. They stopped, not apprehensive and for no more reason than they had first run. The sorrel was available and I put him down. Then I saw a male calf and shot that too before the does fled from the scene to safety.

My two stricken beasts lay on the drilled corn. "Job done!" I said to myself, although as always with fallow deer the shot marks the end of the sport and the beginning of the work. That morning the work included a double session on the drag rope as each beast had to be recovered to the field edge- fortunately down hill all the way – for collection. It was awkward, uncomfortable work on recently cultivated heavy land clods, on which care was required to avoid turning an ankle.

In another corner of this field I erected my Ash Tree High Seat, which was to become another favourite culling place. Once again, this was just my side of the boundary between Twenty Wood and a derelict paddock belonging to the sanctuary. This high seat had several interesting characteristics. First, there was just ten yards to the left of it a footpath along the side of the wood. Whilst it was not heavily walked at least during the hours that I was occupying this high seat, now and then a walker would pass by invariably quite oblivious of my presence above them. Most of these seemed to be doing something- presumably making or taking calls on their mobile phones and blackberries but almost all of them were quite unaware of what was going on around them in the natural world. Each of these geeks – as I understand they are called – demonstrated how people have become so remote and detached from the countryside that most of them might just as well take a walk on a walking machine.

It was possible to see a short distance into Eve's wood from this high seat and so I always kept an eye open for a deer inside the wood as well as outside on the field or, as was more likely coming in off the sanctuary land. One evening, I heard a noise in the wood to my back right and turned my head slightly in time to see an old fallow doe passing by just within it. She appeared to be leading a small group of other fallow although I had no opportunity to assess these. This old doe gave every sign of extreme wariness even whilst she was behind the natural screen provided by the trees. As I was so close and so visible had she just looked up she would have seen me for sure. I had to keep as still as a statue. The doe led her group a few yards further on. I got the impression she then stopped and inspected the field and open ground for possible danger. She then came out and I shot her without waiting for her followers to show. I judged that as she was so close, she would likely see or wind me as she stepped further in front of me and would spook and take her followers with her. She turned into the shot and ran back into the wood. That gave me what I call a woodland stalker's moment and that sinking feeling in which the stalker groans and says under his breath: "I really can't have missed that!"

In this case, it took me a few moments to descend to the ground and enter the wood by way of the gap through which I had, only a minute or two before, been watching the fallow. I walked a few yards further and cast about before finding the doe at the foot of an oak tree thirty yards away. She was without doubt a wary old lady and I felt well satisfied to have added her to the cull list. I hoped that in her absence some of her companions might become easier to approach and cull.

On the other side of the same high seat the naturally favoured deer path between Eve's wood and the sanctuary was the brew of the bank underneath the one hundred and fifty yard long hedge that there separated Eve land from the sanctuary, From the Ash Tree seat, I could see the whole length of this hedge , and of course spent much time watching it. Not infrequently a fallow deer or muntjac would come through the hedge bottom, first head then neck, shoulders and his or her whole body. Although I had a view of this from the seat, a large round branch immediately to my left prevented me from firing off the left hand rail. On seeing the deer here it was necessary to kneel on the seat and engage the deer from the rest provided by the branch, and an awkward one it was too. Fortunately, on the several occasions I tried this, I got away with my gymnastics undetected and grassed the target beast. I had a hunch that these deer were slightly less wary at this place because they had already committed themselves to crossing open ground after presumably making their usual meticulous inspection of the scene. My Ash Tree high seat gave the opportunity of varied shots and was a productive place. On one remarkable evening, when the field in front was half harvested and half standing corn my most assiduous stalking guest accounted for three prickets from it in the course of a short evening. In that same crowded hour I also shot two from the Sunset stand. With the recovery and larder work that ensued, we were late home that evening.

If I have emphasised the culling of our fallow prickets from seats and stands it is because this is the way that most of them were shot. My methodology was to get to a seat before any action was expected and wait there until it did or at least in the hope that it would. I adopted this approach because it was successful often enough to merit the waiting time. The walk and stalk approach did not work as well and often resulted in beasts being seen and spooked or, I suspected, more often making off unseen. The presence of the does in Eve's woods was also a negative factor during the buck cull as the does were much sharper and more likely to detect a still hunting deerstalker than were the prickets that sometimes accompanied them. Now and then of course I, or one of my companions, would have a session still hunting and this would sometimes be productive early on an August or September morning when all or at least some of the cereal crops were standing. Contrary to the accepted wisdom on the subject, windy days could also yield a chance with the wind noise disguising the approach of the deerstalker to deer tucked up and concentrated in a sheltered corner or behind a thick hedge.

The strategy was then to achieve the bulk of the fallow buck cull before the opening of the doe season on 1 November. In detail, I aimed to get the numbers in August and September when the prickets would be vulnerable by reason of their need to leave the sanctuary and prowl the fields, and the advantage I had at that season from both the concealment and feed provided by the standing crops. The quality of the prickets culled in the early autumn was excellent and prime carcases became available for the table or for sale to the game dealer. The other benefit of this timing was that the woods on Eve could be left quiet during the month of October, which encouraged my fallow does to stay or become resident. I know that there is a school of thought in deer management that says it is not worth shooting the male fallow and that the main effort should be directed against the does- the breeding machines of the herd. This simply did not apply to my situation with the does living in the adjoining sanctuary. The does were hefted to the sanctuary and could only be caught up with and culled on the Eve estate land in occasional careless moments and certainly not as a matter of course. So, the culling of prickets definitely assisted in the tree and crop protection so badly needed on Eve, and, in my opinion, was definitely worth doing.

During the many years I conducted this pricket cull I complied with my original instructions in a meticulous manner and am proud to say that no stand fallow buck was ever shot. They were all left unmolested and I have a treasure house of wonderful memories involving these great beasts. I watched a massive common fallow buck one afternoon on the woodland edge. He was gorging himself on windfall crab apples and I watched with delight as, the better to swallow the apples, he lifted his head high. Every time he swept back his magnificent racks I gasped with disbelief at the size and symmetry of them. On another warm late summer evening, a big black buck stepped out of the wood no more than fifty yards to the right of my high seat. Accompanied by a young buck, he grazed in the standing wheat and I watched him with pleasure until he became a dark shape in the fast fading light and eventually disappeared into the darkness.

On one deer moving day, which was conducted in a cold snap-snow on the ground and sub-zero temperature- I entered a wood by way of a half acre stand of laurel bushes which, in turn merged with a compartment comprising a thicket of young coppice and bramble. Coming into this, I turned out a magnificent buck from under a bush. At close quarters, and with a grunt of displeasure, he unwound himself from the warmth and comfort of his bed and made directly towards the blind occupied by the waiting rifle. He was a cheerful young soldier, not long back from foreign parts and, as the buck made to exit the wood, I remembered to my horror that I had forgotten to warn him off "trophy bucks". I put my hands in my ears dreading to hear the shot that would notify me of the consequences of my slackness, but no shot was discharged.

A few minutes later I emerged to find an ecstatic young officer, over the moon with the close up view he had had of this big fellow. The big buck had come to the woodland edge and stood in front of the high seat and this young Rifle had remembered my instructions from his previous visits a year before. This was particularly creditable as in the months since he had last been on the Estate, he had been out in much rough weather and had experienced many dangerous moments.

On a couple of occasions, guest rifles culled promising young bucks which would have been better left. Although sad to see a young buck floored before his time, I never made a fuss about these mistakes. Having observed and studied so many heads myself, I am only too well aware that it is easy to misjudge one. This is of course particularly true when the deerstalker is still hunting in bad light. He is then likely to have a meeting engagement with a buck, perhaps at a ride junction or in the shade of some trees. He has a moment to decide whether it is safe to shoot and another whether or not to engage him. The whole process happens so swiftly that there is no possibility of undertaking the studied assessment which, more often than not, can and should be made by the deerstalker who is concealed in a high seat, and whose quarry is likely to be unaware of his presence. The advantages of a high seat or ground blind in selective shooting is a point that my experienced German stalking friend, Carl Wiers, has often made to me, although he concedes that walking and stalking in the early mornings is a most enjoyable way in which to hunt.

Chapter Eleven

Small Barking Deer

I READ ABOUT MUNTJAC long before I stalked them. That master hunter, Jim Corbett, mentioned the muntjac in his books as, now and then, one would bark in the jungle and warn Corbett of the whereabouts of a tiger. In his memoir "The Jungle is Neutral" the remarkable and resourceful Freddie Spencer Chapman touches on his hunting experiences against muntjac in Malaya and there describes the susceptibility of muntjac to a high pitched call made from bamboo. I believe the now widely used practice of calling muntjac in English woodland derives from Chapman's account of it and I will refer to this again later in this chapter. Corbett recorded how muntjac were despised by many people as a cowardly, small animal but how he, Corbett, had some admiration for them. He showed me that they had a place in the scheme of things in the Indian jungle and, though his example, I regarded them with an open mind when I first encountered them here.

My first experiences with muntjac were at Peninsular Farm. At that time the large adjoining woodland blocks were lightly stalked, if at all. They had come to harbour a significant population of these small deer. These had taken to coming on to Peninsular Farm to feed on the growing crops and also on the plants, flowers and shrubs in the gardens of the local houses, and their depredations during these visits made them unpopular. The farmer who owned Peninsular Farm and the adjoining home owners were, by the time I arrived on the scene, mainly in agreement that the only good muntjac was a dead one! I was enthusiastically encouraged to make a heavy cull. I have described above how Peninsular farm was a flat land farm intersected by public footpaths and tracks and with several houses backing on to the south end of it. My first line of attack was to cull from my high seats. As muntjac evidently visited the spinney by the farm buildings, I started there and succeeded in shooting a yearling buck and a doe. The shots were taken at much closer range than was usual for roe and fallow, and I found it necessary to be very alert in the high seat if I was to catch out one of these small deer wandering through the nettles and other vegetation. The proximity of the deer to the high seat, their propensity to look up and their busy, restless way of moving combined to present novel challenges to the deerstalker, which I enjoyed from the start.

Having accounted for these two animals in the spinney, I decided to try the high seat that overlooked the two faces of the adjoining woodland. Whilst sitting in this high seat, I could see over the perimeter hedge into the woodland floor. This resulted in some interesting observations. My view from the high seat into the wood corner was not an unimpeded one as it would have been on an open field, but a series of gaps between the trees which, as it happened, were all mature conifers. In places there was under storey but in others the woodland floor was bare. With the assiduous use of my binoculars, I was able to spy the wood's floor and observe the animals and birds that I saw on it. Quite often, in the course of these outings, I would see muntjac moving about in their busy manner. Sometimes, the muntjac I observed would be a mature buck and as likely as not, he would have about him that aggressive demeanour, that "I'm looking for a fight" mien, so typical of the male of that species. On other occasions, I would get a view of a heavy-in-calf doe muntjac. Her behaviour would be quite different, the epitome of caution and discretion, with the awareness of the mother rather than the aggression of the male. The does with young at heel always presented a charming cameo and I enjoyed watching the youngsters taking instruction from their mothers as they went about their business.

Deer moving from left to right at this spot were all coming from the interior of the wood and so in many cases were intending to come out of the wood through the perimeter hedge and ditch to feed on the fields belonging to Peninsular Farm or to visit the Spinney and nearby houses. When I saw a suitable cull beast making it's way to the edge of the wood I would therefore become optimistic as to my chances of a shot at it. This would lead to some intensely exciting moments of anticipation as I could not follow the complete, uninterrupted path of the muntjac over the woodland floor. My view was too often blocked for that. Sometimes of course the muntjac never did appear on the field outside the wood but more often than not my anticipation would be satisfied by the appearance through the hedge of first a diminutive head and shoulders and then the whole beast. And then it was trigger time!

I was often close to these muntjac- too close sometimes- and had problems in depressing the rifle barrel far enough down to take an accurate shot. A sack filled with straw in the seat gave me more elevation and helped solve that problem. I also found these small deer were very durable. I had by then acquired a .270 in addition to a .243 and, even when accurately shot with a 130 grain bullet from the former, a stricken muntjac would sometimes jump back into the woodland and fall some yards into it, often in thick cover. In the summer time this made retrieval difficult and I adopted the practice, to which I still adhere, of keeping one or more of my gun dogs on stand-by in my truck ready for a search. After one or two problems, I found that the best practice was to take a brief look to see if the beast was lying where it could be seen. If it was not, I would go straight for my dog and cast him off from the point of impact. Usually the muntjac would then be found very quickly and the spoiling or complete loss of the carcass avoided.

Another sporting shot that I enjoyed here was at those muntjac that jumped out of the wood through the hedge on the face of it that ran away from the high seat. I had a view of four hundred yards in this direction and so would frequently see deer emerge. The muntjac liked to pop out and then make their way along the brew of the bank, pausing here and there to graze some tasty morsel. If I was lucky one of these would come near enough for me to engage it, but it would be quite as likely to take fright at some noise from the houses behind me and go back into the wood. With experience indicating that the outcome was never certain and that I just had a sporting chance of a shot, I had to decide when to shoot and whether, in particular circumstances, I should forbear from doing so. I remember one nice buck that prowled along the hedge, coming in well towards me and stopped to feed on the edge of the field at about one hundred yards distance. A clean kill and that one dropped on the drilled corn where he had been standing. No need for a dog that evening!

With the large local population of muntjac deer on my stalking grounds, I soon began to appreciate the efficacy of high seats for culling them. This was particular true of those seats which were situated in or on the edge of woodland and around game covers. My Village High Seat was a prime example of this, being surrounded by bushes and brambles and the reeds of a pond and having in front of it a tasty block of maize. One blank August morning was transformed when a mature muntjac buck appeared as if by magic from the game cover in front of the seat. He stepped out with a bold assurance, but no doubt had stood in the edge of the maize for a good long look round before emerging. Once outside in the open, he headed for the nearest cover at a smart pace. As he was in my killing zone, I called out "Hey!" As always, I called quite loudly as there is nothing more infuriating than seeing a target muntjac continuing and walking out of the killing field. This one stopped immediately and I was able to shoot him in the base of the neck.

On another morning, this time during a cold snap the winter I walked along the edge of another maize strip, but separated from it by a recently coppiced hedge and ditch and an unmown grass strip. The land sloped gently towards the reed bed I have described earlier. I went very slowly, trying to stalk every step of the way, with the breeze blowing into my left cheek. There was an open fallow field to my right so I was able to ignore this and concentrate on the cover to my left. I made frequent and extensive use of my binoculars. I felt certain I would see roe or muntjac deer but, in that situation, thought it likely they would see me first. As it was, I was within twenty yards of the end of the cover before I glimpsed a muntjac. It disappeared almost immediately but in such a way that I did not think he had got me. I could shoot over the hedge, without the shot being obstructed, so I set up my stalking sticks where I was and rested the rifle in the fork of them. I was in the long grass, half hidden by the short hedge.

I was looking into the maize which, by this time in the winter had many broken stalks and gaps in it. I waited in the expectation that I would see that muntjac again. He must have walked towards me because when next I did see him, he was just the other side of the hedge, really too close for comfort. Depressing the rifle barrel, I allowed an inch or two to take account of the exceptionally close range, the danger being that the shot would go high. I didn't even try for the neck but opted for a shot aimed at the middle of the chest. At the shot, the little deer jumped and disappeared into the maize. I reloaded quickly and it was a good thing I did as, a few moments later, a doe muntjac showed in precisely the same place. I shot her too and she dropped where she stood. I jumped the ditch and, after a short search in the cover crop, retrieved the buck from the small clearing in which it had collapsed. That was another brace to be added to the credit side of the cull list.

Having originally thought a misnomer the term "still hunting" as used to describe walking whilst stalking or, more precisely, stalking whilst walking, I soon revised my opinion by redefining it as "walking so slowly whilst stalking that the stalker seems to be standing still."

The geography of Bourn Valley Farms in places lent itself particularly well to still hunting. Whilst it was true that there were some large arable fields, devoid of all but transient deer, the small woods and plantations connected by a network of hedges and ditches all provided attractive habitat to muntjac and the temptation for them to go walkabout. On recognising this tendency, I began to exploit it. My method was to set out on foot with my rifle and sticks. I would carry my rifle loaded- on safe of course- and be ready to shoot as soon as a safe shot at a suitable muntjac presented itself. I would have my extending bipod stalking sticks at their full length so as to enable me to take a standing shot. This was desirable as it would give me a better, safer background by increasing the angle of the shot into the ground. I also carried a lightweight plastic bipod which I could clip on to the rifle barrel. This was a useful aid in taking longer shots from prone. Such chances were not very common but by using the short bipod when they did I could extend my effective range and shoot more reliably.

I remember one May morning when the grass was beginning to grow. I had left my vehicle in the farmyard and walked down the road with a view to approaching the Bourn Valley Farms reed bed from the north- the wind was south, south westerly. There was just space for me to slip into the first field from the road by the side of a farm gate. Here there was a slight rise in the ground and, on cresting this, I knew I would have a view over the best part of an acre of rough grass and also the edge of a small portion of the reed bed. Although adjacent to the road, the spot was a discreet one in the early hours of a May morning, and favoured by both roe and muntjac deer.

I was in luck that morning. There was a young muntjac buck in the grass. When I first spied him, he had his head down and was facing away from me partly concealed. I set the sticks up, getting a lean off the fork in them. I got the cross hairs of the rifle scope on to the buck, which was still feeding with his back towards me and waited. Then the buck started to move, heading towards the reeds. He had pulled out the distance further than was ideal when he stopped and turned and enabled me to engage him. There were a few shade giving willow trees and a dyke with water in it so I performed a field gralloch and hung the muntjac on a branch in one of these trees. I thought it would be fly free there until I had finished stalking. Washing my hands and arms and my knife, I continued my stalk by creeping along the side of the reed bed.

There was that morning much of interest to see and hear. As I am always inclined to stalk too fast, I concentrated hard on creeping along the edge of the cover, and made sure I stopped every few yards to glass my surroundings. I made myself say that I must stalk so slowly I would not seem to be moving. After proceeding for some distance in this fashion, I came to a ditch that served to drain the fields on the slope to my right and sat for some minutes on the bank of this. This was something of a vantage point and I carefully glassed all parts of the farm that I could see from here. There were a great number of game birds and also hares and rabbits going about their affairs in an unhurried and undisturbed manner.

Shortly after I moved on, the habitat began to change with the reeds being replaced by a watercourse either side of which were trees and other cover. These led to a larger wood, which I knew offered me the likely prospect of another shot. This was on my mind as I drew closer to the wood, so I told myself on no account to hotspot. It was so easy to bump a deer before you get to where they are most likely to be if you stop stalking and start hurrying. That was a good call as there was a roe doe round the next corner and, as she was unaware of me, I was able to wait for a few minutes and allow her to graze off. I wondered whether she had a buck with her, but did not see him if he was there. Going on slowly, I spotted a yearling muntjac doe by a bramble bush on the woodland edge. I needed to get in closer and managed to make an approach by using the cover to mask my movement. Another shot off the sticks was required here and she joined the buck in the bag.

After this, there was time to visit one more regular spy point, where I sat in the ditch by the badger set and viewed a fine expanse of country in the coming May sunshine. This was a spot from which I had happy memories of prone shots taken off my short bipod; it was a favourite place. As I glassed the scene, I saw the first dog walker of the morning and realised my stalking was over. Getting up, I picked up my muntjac doe, which was no great weight and made my way back to collect the buck before heading home after what I considered to be a first rate morning's sport. I had many such mornings in Bourn Valley doing useful culling and, at the same time, enjoying myself enormously. In due course, I was to apply a similar technique to muntjac control at Eve.

From the beginning of my involvement in low ground deer management, I had stalked in both the morning and evening, although with rather more success in the morning. In the Bourn Valley and Maytree Farms the heavy level of walking and other disturbances was probably responsible for this with evening outings, even if not being completely wrecked, being spoiled by a walker off the path or a wild dog off it's lead and running wild. Whatever the reason, I much favoured morning outings. However, when I started stalking at Eve my early morning starts became even earlier by reason of the journey from my home to the Estate. Whilst I did not have any difficulty in getting up and out before first light, in high summer this involved a 3a.m. start and the effect of this was detrimental to my practice of law later in the day and sixty miles away, and two such mornings in a row would preclude the practice of law at all. It was plain I would have to concentrate more of my stalking outings into the evenings in the summer time if I was to combine the attainment of my cull targets with my professional life as a solicitor. As things turned out, that was the start of some wonderful still hunting for muntjac on Eve.

The large size of Eve, and it's historical links with the conservation of game meant that it had on it many hedges and belts which, when they came on the scene, muntjac found very much to their liking. Once the cereal, beans and rape were standing there were acres of cover and feed and the little deer had thrived. I would aim to arrive at Eve by 6 or 7p.m. on a summer evening to start still hunting. Selecting a start point that would give me an evening's stalking with the wind in my face, I would set off with rifle, stick and binoculars and, in addition, a large roe sack. I would not always need this- low ground stalking is just not like that- but more often than not this was very useful.

One evening, before the start of harvest on the heavy land farms, I parked my truck in a meadow and set out on foot on a route that took me past the gateway into one of the woods. There, within two minutes of starting, I came on the unusual sight of a muntjac buck deeply asleep in the middle of the main ride. I said a grateful thank you for this good fortune and shot him. Rather than carry his carcass for the rest of the evening, I took it back to the truck where it would be uncontaminated by flies. After the short time that this took, I resumed my walk. As I reflected on my kill, I thought that some might say I had been unsporting and unduly hard nosed to shoot that buck whilst he was asleep. If that was so then my answer to it was that I had a job to do for the Eve Estate owners. I drew the line at shooting muntjac does with fawns at heel, or those that gave the appearance of having just calved, but I regarded any other muntjac as fair game regardless of whether he or she was asleep or awake.

Making my way along a hedge, I walked for a fifty yard stretch and then stopped and observed before progressing for a further fifty yards and so on. In this I made much use of my binoculars and swept not only the bottom of the hedge but the margin and the edge of the standing crop which, at that point, was wall to wall wheat. Although the many acres of cover could have hidden a lot of muntjac, I was not unduly worried by this as the vicinity of the hedge, grass margin and crop edge was the location favoured by the small deer. Unless they wanted a change of scenery, they had little need to move out into the middle of the wheat fields. On this evening, my dogged progress went unrewarded and at length I reached the face of a large wood on Eve Estate's northern boundary. At this point, the hedge on my left was replaced by the forest edge and my hopes were enhanced.

Straight away I saw two deer and these were a fallow doe and calf. I stood still and watched them grazing in the edge of the wheat. They were both feeding in a hungry way and, at the same time, swishing their tails to deter the flies that were obviously bothering them. I could do nothing but stand still and watch them until, having evidently fed well, they turned and went back into the forest and immediately out of sight. That was typical of fallow, I thought. At one moment they were there, as bold as brass, and the next they were gone as if they had never been there. Anyway, their departure freed up my route and I prowled the forest edge for another three hundred yards without seeing a hair. That brought me to one of my high seats and I climbed up into it so that I could the better survey the forest edge and fields beyond. There was another distant fallow doe standing in the corn and, I got the impression, more of her species in the forest edge. She constantly kept lifting her head and looking back there. They were obstructing my route and my options narrowed down to two. I could stay where I was in the high seat or get down and follow the nearby hedge that ran away from the forest. Although I thought the first option the better of the two, I felt in the mood for a walk and, with the long evening light, had every chance of a meeting engagement with another muntjac. Not for the first time I felt the conflict that comes from surrendering a proven high seat for a spot of still hunting, but nonetheless decided to go for it.

Resuming my stalk, I padded along the hedge with the forest now at my back and the wind, such as it was, in my left cheek. The hedge stalk was uneventful and took me over a lane and on towards a square, scruffy near derelict little wood, an old orchard if it's name was anything to go by. Watching this carefully for some minutes led to my spotting a discreet movement in the box bushes on the woodland edge, followed by the emergence of another buck muntjac. I added him to the bag and, in the gloaming, turned to commence my long walk back towards the truck. The wind was in my back now and so I walked briskly along the lane. I had done stalking for that night.

I have enjoyed many such evenings. These became and remain a feature of my summer time stalking. I always enthused about setting out with rifle and shooting sticks for an armed stroll looking for nothing more than a breeze in my face and a chance encounter with a small barking deer. On occasion, I stalked into roe and fallow and, if these were in season and on my cull list, would take one of these. Such opportunities were, however, a bonus on evenings dedicated to my relentless pursuit of the muntjac.

In the early years that I pursued the muntjac my modes of hunting were limited to still hunting- with an emphasis on these summer evening prowls- and to waiting in high or low seats. These were productive methods and I was pleased to observe that my efforts thinned out the numbers of these small deer. I was given to understand that the owners of the Eve Estate were pleased too. However, Eve was a large estate, with a considerable amount of favourable habitat and cover for muntjac, and the business of culling them was a slow one- as indeed is most low ground deer culling. Ideally, I needed another, less time consuming modus operandi.

I was to find exactly what I wanted in a wartime memoir entitled "The Jungle Is Neutral" by Lt. Col. F.S. Chapman. This is not the place to dwell on the Second World War exploits of Freddie Spencer Chapman. Suffice to say, he was an exceptional man and a hero in the true sense of that now abused word. Chapman spent much of the War in occupied Malaya (as it was then) where he lived in guerrilla camps. In addition to his military duties, he constantly studied the natural history of the jungle and recorded this. He also spent much time hunting, often on his own but on occasion with the local native Sakai hunters. It was from the Sakai that Chapman learnt how to call muntjac by using a bamboo call which made a high pitched sound. Chapman said this was so effective that it was rather unsporting, which shows the quality of the man when one considers he was

Roe buck in April ground elder

An April culling field

May cull - muntjac and roe

Summer ride

At the muntjac

Young roe buck at rut time

Round the mulberry bush!

Harvest prickett

Recovering the carcass

Autumn evening

Trigger time!

Fallow fraying

Deerstalker and dog

Winter view

Cold weather ambush

Glassing the woodland edge

Enduring fray damage

A morning's work

Snow under sunshine

Fallow tracks

Snow doe

Snow pricket

December deer pond

February roe doe

Late winter ride

Muntjac buck - February

Yearling fallow - March

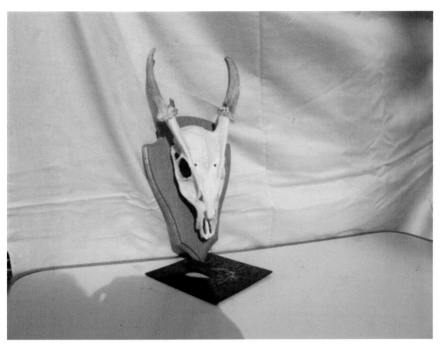

An exceptional trophy

Curved racks - Muntjac

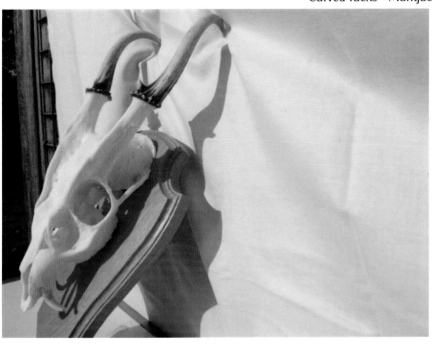

A malform

dependent on the animals he shot, if not for all his food, at least for a varied diet.

I am ashamed to say I had no such reservations when I decided to try calling muntjac myself. I had previously practised the then much more widely art of roe buck calling and possessed a number of roe calls including one commercially marketed as a Buttolo Universal Roe Call. This call has two plastic reeds on it secured by aluminium clips. When blown, the thinner of these strips or reeds, produces a high pitched sound intended to imitate a distressed roe doe kid calling it's mother. The call generated by blowing the wider reed at the opposite end has a lower pitch being supposedly an imitation of the call made by a roe deer doe to entice a roe buck during the rut. At that time I had no knowledge of the design of the Sakai call or even what part of the bamboo plant was used. It seemed entirely possible that bamboo leaves could have been used to make a call in the same way as beech leaves are by European roe deer stalkers. However, it was also perfectly feasible that small parts of the ubiquitous bamboo canes and stems could have been fashioned into a tool for the job.

As I had a number of calls designed to attract roe deer and foxes I decided to start with these. I remember my first attempt very well. On Bourn Valley Farms, the biggest wood was on the side of a hill and was very tricky to stalk in a conventional way. On the bottom side of it, there was often stock and the topside consisted of a raised lip, which meant that any shot at an emergent deer would have been sky lined. There were however deer living in this wood and I had, many years previously, called my first roe deer buck in it in my first season of stalking. I resolved to try calling for muntjac there.

That June morning, I went very quietly into the bottom of the wood. There was a stand of ancient yew trees there and the shade of their branches restricted the under storey to ground elder having a height of six to nine inches and some clumps of box bushes. With some difficulty I found a suitable yew tree that was sparsely branched. I needed a tree trunk that I could back up against for cover and a view from it of the woodland floor in front of me and a clear or at least reasonably clear lane of fire. Only deerstalkers who have had to select such spots will really appreciate how difficult it is to pick an effective stand. It is so easy to get it wrong, as some of the incidents recorded in this book show all too well. On this first attempt, I stood backed up to the yew tree trunk. A few yards behind me was the wood edge and below it the cattle field. There were cattle in it so I would not be shooting that way. In front of me there was a patch of ground elder perhaps half the size of a tennis court. This was flanked by box bushes, which I judged would likely mask anything within them. I thought that if I had the opportunity of a shot, it would be at a muntjac deer in the square of ground elder immediately in front of me , a safe, clear killing place if I could ever get a muntjac to come out of the bushes into it.

I went about my first muntjac calling attempt as if I was roe calling. Having found a stand, I waited for several minutes to let the wood settle down and forget the disturbance occasioned by my arrival. As I was always impatient at this point I resorted to my usual trick of visualising deer and game birds standing in the undergrowth , head cocked, listening intently for further noise, having perhaps half heard the brush of a twig against my coat or the rustle of leaves under my boot. I imagined them listening, assessing the possible threat, and then, satisfied there was none, putting their heads down to browse and feed or lying down again in their woodland beds. After ten minutes, I set up my shooting sticks and rested the rifle on them. I then began to call. The resulting screech sounded very loud in the enclosed woodland surroundings. I repeated it half a dozen times when, to my surprise, there was a noise in the box bushes followed by the rapid appearance in the clearing of a fine muntjac buck. He bounced out and nearly up to me before recoiling and running back to the edge of the clearing. He held there for a moment, long enough anyway for me to drop him where he stood. I walked forward to him with shaking hands. I had shot my first muntjac buck to the call.

My development of muntjac calling as a strategy for culling them followed this first experience at Bourn Valley Farm. Many other interesting incidents were to occur whilst I was calling there and elsewhere.

On another summer afternoon at Clay Farm, I was calling muntjac in a wood managed for pheasant shooting. Shaped like a slice of cheese, there was a flushing area situated about seventy five yards from the front of this, where the woodland floor was kept clear of cover at all times. By taking up a stand facing this, with my back to the direction of the drive, I had an unusually good view of this bare area. I crept in past the gun stands, remembering as I did so the good times I had enjoyed at these whilst pheasant shooting over the years. Creeping into the wood, I made it to the flushing area without, as far as I could tell, disturbing any deer. On starting to call, I soon had no less than four agitated muntjac in front of me. No doubt the doe was in season and that was the explanation for the presence of her entourage. If these bucks liked her, they certainly didn't like each other. The movement of these deer was so hectic that it was impossible to interpret what was happening. Whilst I would have liked to observe the interplay between the various beasts and their continuing reaction to the call, I needed to be culling and had to terminate the study session with a shot as soon as I could select a standing still buck in the melee.

That was not the only time I called more than one muntjac at a time and in fact I began to think that the more muntjac were present, the more readily they would respond to my call, particularly when there was a doe in season in the wood.

For each occasion on which a muntjac bounced out of cover in response to the call there were three or four on which he or she or they (as the case might be) would come in much more cautiously.

There was an excellent wood for calling on Eve, a rectangular wood on a slope, the lower side of which had enough clear under storey under a compartment of yew trees to allow a shot of up to forty yards if I sat at the foot of one of these trees. A call here, only made after I was sitting still with the rifle on shortened sticks, would often bring in a muntjac. One morning, whilst calling, I caught a glimpse of movement in the nettles up the hill and then watched a young doe strolling towards my position whilst trying to pretend she was not interested, and that she just just happened to be walking my way. I didn't call again after seeing her- too much in her face to be credible I thought- but it turned out there was no need. She kept coming in and I let her come until she was standing in front of a tree when I engaged her.

In the course of another morning calling session, I had too much cover to contend with and the chance of a shot restricted to the open ride between two compartments of the wood. I didn't like calling there at all as the likely outcome would be one or more muntjac approaching through the thicket, ascertaining what was happening and then withdrawing having unwittingly been educated by myself. However, it was a case of needs must when the devil drives, as there was no other suitable place in the wood from which to call. As it turned out the outcome of my calling was the appearance and culling of a doe muntjac on the ride. No sooner had she been accounted for than a muntjac buck stated to bark on my left and, as was clear from the direction of the bark, he was circling my position unsettled and alert but not actually spooked and not making off. He carried on like this for some minutes during which I was straining for a glimpse of him through the undergrowth, mainly young sycamore here, and hearing but not seeing him. At last he worked round far enough to get a whiff of wind and backed off into the deep recesses of the wood. I was irritated by his escape as I rightly reckoned it would be a long time before he answered my call again.

That had been a good morning for calling with a touch of warmth and a silky breeze. Although I found muntjac most responsive in those summery conditions, I also sometimes experienced success at calling them in the winter months. The advantage of the technique was, first, that it could be quickly deployed in a spinney or small wood in which the deerstalker would be reluctant to risk wasting a full sitting up session. It was, secondly, highly effective and a great aid to the deer manger concerned to achieve his cull. Finally, it was satisfying to select the culling ground, get in to it and call and cull successfully. If, for any particular reason, I did not wish to cull a called muntjac then I could and would pass up the shot. This particularly applied to muntjac does which either had, or were likely to have, dependent kids. The incidents I have described are only examples of numerous experiences I had whilst calling, and impressed themselves on me as sporting stalking for muntjac deer. I found there was no certainty that muntjac would come to the call, and that the experience was far more chancy than calling roe deer during their rut.

Chapter Twelve

The Female of the Species

I MAY SO FAR have given the impression that my deer stalking quarry comprised wholly or at any rate mainly male roe and fallow deer. Far from this being the case, I recognised from the start that not only would I have to cull female deer but that in places this would be the most important part of my cull. I remember a discussion I had with a game shot in the Bourn Valley who was against me shooting does on the basis that by so doing I was damaging my future sport with the bucks. I did not agree with that. First, even if it had been possible, it was not my intention to shoot out the does in the Bourn Valley. It was rather to keep the numbers of male and female deer to a reasonable figure that all concerned – farmers, foresters, game keepers and local residents- could tolerate and enjoy. In order to achieve this or something like it was vital for me to shoot some does.

I soon discovered that this was no easy task. I was reluctant to shoot roe does with dependent fawns before Christmas because it seemed too early to be orphaning them. The sight of one or two fawns on their own in January and February illustrated that. In those days that left January and February available to do the cull- the month of March having only recently been added. However, there was much pheasant shooting going on over my ground in January and pigeon shooting in February, which combined to make it unavailable, or the subject of disturbance that was detrimental to culling. Then there was the probability of bad weather which, when it happened, inhibited deer movement. In practice I discovered that there was only a small window of opportunity for roe doe culling and that achieving the planned number of doe culls required focused effort. After a couple of experimental seasons, I settled on two methods. First, I would stalk roe does, in a similar manner to my roe buck stalking, although I would often invite guest stalkers to get more rifles on the ground. Secondly, I arranged deer moving days when I would attempt to move deer forward to concealed rifles.

My roe doe stalking provided me with some fine sporting moments and incidents involving me in incidents variously amusing, challenging or just very satisfying. One winter an extended family of seven roe deer took to feeding on a drilled wheat field beside the bourn. These deer were to be seen grazing there very regularly and, having been undisturbed, often lay down in the open to ruminate. I thought that I might be able to approach these deer by stalking them down the bed of the bourn. At shortly after 2.30p.m.on a bitterly cold January afternoon I slid down the bank into the bourn nearly half a mile from these deer. I began to make my way downstream and, before going very far, realised I was going to suffer wet feet, as the water was higher than the wellington boots I was wearing. Once wet, there was nothing for it but to put up with the discomfort and to continue my stalk. For much of the time, the banks of the bourn were sufficiently high to conceal my movements, but I had to be careful in places not to show myself. If even my head was likely to give me away, I would crouch down and duck walk as best I could. I became even wetter when I tried this.

Now and then I peeped cautiously over the bank and was pleased to see all the deer in the group were lying down in that characteristic back to back style that roe deer adopt in the cold. I observed, less happily, that three of the deer were facing in my direction. Continuing to head downstream, I eventually came to a stoway which comprised a track over a giant pipe. In order to achieve a firing position, I had to either negotiate the stoway or crawl through the pipe. It was January and the usual vegetation that grows on the banks of the bourn was absent .The track over it was overlooked by three of the roe deer in the group. I decided I had no chance of getting in "over the top". Shouldering my rifle in such a way that it was horizontal, I got down on my hands and knees at the entrance to the pipe. The stream water was cold and uncomfortable as it at once soaked my breeks nearly up to the waist band. Shuffling forward, I worked my way through the pipe sections, rather disliking the curious sensation produced by the effect of being in the water with the pipe otherwise enveloping me. I was glad to emerge at the other end, although by now teeth chatteringly cold from my unwanted bath.

The roe deer were still in the field, and evidently unaware of my approach. Taking my time, I kept in the streambed until I was opposite them. Then, I had a little luck, as I came on a hollow created by a partial collapse of the bank. I got into this and found that it, being by chance the right height, gave me a perfect opportunity for a shot off the bipod. As one of the does was lying away from the others, and had the back of her head to me, I shot her there where she lay and, in the confusion that followed, also accounted for a calf.

I was very pleased with the design and execution of that stalk. In a sport which supplies endless opportunities for the stalker to get things wrong or just for things to go wrong, I was ecstatic that I had got it all right and grateful for the good lady luck who had smiled on my scheme. In gralloching the mature doe by the water's edge, I found twin foetuses inside her. As ever, the culling of a doe carrying young caused me a twinge of sadness. That was the moment, as a deerstalker, I had to remember there was a job to be done, and another doe to be culled.

Observation of winter roe taught me that in December, January and the first half of February, their movement was generally very limited. Whilst not true to say they were hibernating, the deer were in severe weather and short day modes. The winter weather of course varied but I knew when I didn't see them and that was when there was rain or snow. On frosty mornings they were likely to stay bedded down until the sun came up, if it ever did. When they did move, they preferred not to move far. I suspect it was no accident that this lack of movement coincided with the shortest days of the year. With so few hours of daylight, they could sit them out and emerge to feed in the comparative safety of darkness. Later, with shorter nights, the deer would be forced from cover by hunger, whilst it was still light.

I culled one of these New Year roe does by exploiting their use of rough grass and young trees for bedding down. Having previously put up a high seat, I went into it well before first light- that's at about 7a.m. then - and waited for the light to come. I saw nothing until just before 8a.m., in a much improved light by then, when I saw three roe, buck, doe and follower. I say I saw them; really what I saw was bits of them. With roe being the small deer they are and blending in with their surroundings as they do in the winter, it took time and effort with the binoculars to ascertain which was which and then to try to avoid them becoming muddled up again. Even at short range these deer kept disappearing behind screens of grass and tree guards, or into blind spots and hollows. They were in no hurry and it took them some time to graze through the young trees and grass to a spot where I could essay a clear shot. Then, when I did have a chance, it was at the doe kid and I took her but never had a chance at the old doe. She ran off with the buck.

Having got down from my high seat and walked over to where the young doe ought to have been, she wasn't there. I spent a few minutes searching with increasing anxiety before pulling out and going back to my truck for my labrador, Bison. I slipped his lead on and walked him to the supposed point of shot. I released him there with my usual instruction to him to " find the buck!" and he cast about for a scent in all that rough, disappearing himself now and then behind clumps of tall, winter pale clumps of grass. After a short spell of steady circling he stopped out of sight and, when I saw him again, I could see his tail wagging. Going over to him, I found him licking the exit wound behind the doe's shoulder and praised him for finding my beast. As usual Bison was less impressed by that than the prospect of a roe deer heart, which a few minutes later he was happily scoffing.

One miserable, cold, wet winter I became fed up by early February with the difficulties of culling or more accurately attempting to cull roe deer at Eve that wouldn't move much and, if in my woods at all, hung on in the thickets through all or most of the daylight hours. On the 14 February I decided to have a change of scenery in the form of an evening outing to Bourn Valley Farms. There was a southerly wind and, no sooner was I out on the ground than I became conscious

90

of the mildness of the day and the pulling out of the daylight hours. On my last visit in January, the light, such as it was, had been failing by 3.00p.m. Now, at the same hour, it was still strong and I felt quite exposed as I climbed into the fork of my favourite oak tree. I had an enjoyable afternoon there as just the hint of spring was making the local birds and mammals active and a couple of cock pheasants were sparring in the paddock adjacent to the watercourse.

And then, as I had been so confident I would, I saw her. I saw the old doe standing just inside the wood. I watched her looking out, inspecting and assessing the scene. I caught a glimpse of another beast in the wood and then a white tush. Although the light was still good, the lead doe could wait no longer and walked out of the wood with her two companions line astern. Following her lead, the three grey animals crossed in front of me heading, I thought, for the field with the best bite on it. It was exciting to watch and to have this harbinger of spring with it's enhanced chance of productive culling weather.

I waited for the lead doe to come into my killing zone, the position in which I would simply have to raise the rifle and engage her with the minimum of movement. I waited; I didn't blink or shuffle. I watched her from under the peak of my cap, gloved hands on the rifle, rifle on branch rest.

Then she and her companions put their heads up sharply and held them watching something or someone behind me. They watched, decided they didn't like it and took off in leaps and bounds for the safety of the wood. After they had gone in, I looked behind me and saw the farmer's familiar truck. Oh no! ; it's not just deer and deer stalkers who enjoy a spring afternoon.

Another vivid recollection concerns the badger hedge doe. There is, in one remote corner of Eve a badger set in the vicinity of which I have had several sightings of badgers. Whilst stalking, I have seen then heading out in the evening and returning in the dawn. I am often amazed by the fast speed at which badgers cover the ground. One amusing encounter took place as I walked past the sett in the early hours of a summer morning. A big boar badger was busy in the main entrance. Head down the hole, he didn't hear me and I was able to study his rear end for some time, which gave me an unusual nature study period. Much to my shame, I cannot even now give an accurate description of a badger's back side.

On the far side of the badger hedge there was a small half moon shaped field, enclosed by a boundary hedge on the high side of it. Mid-February in this particular year a group of roe started using this field. I saw them first from a fairly distant wood and then saw them frequently. They were regulars and day after day I saw them either lying or grazing on the wheat crop that had been sown in the autumn that small field. As the corner field was within Eve's boundary, I was not able to stalk into it from the north, east or west, which limited my options and for that same reason would not be able to attain and exploit the high ground. Whilst in that part of the estate, I worried away at finding a solution to the problem of approaching these roe deer. In the end I decided a long crawl behind the badger hedge was my only chance and that's what I essayed one windy afternoon with the beasts lying out in the thin February sunshine. The crawling was a mixture of hands and knees and leopard stuff and was very dirty on that wet, heavy land. By the time I had achieved a firing point I was covered in a patina of clay as was all my equipment.

I had to take the bolt out of my rifle to check the muzzle had not become obstructed with soil during the stalk. Then, after replacing it and reloading, it was necessary for me to stand up and shoot off the hedge top in order to have the bullet, if it missed the deer, go into the hill. A shot off my short bipod would have had an inadequate background.

My target doe and her cohort were getting agitated by this performance, all by then being on their feet and making ready to go out over the boundary. I had to be quick and was. That really was a rare stalk in which the walk back loaded with roe a deer doe was a great deal more pleasant than the stalk there. It's one thing to crawl on the heather hill at stag time; but quite another on a heavy land ploughed field in February.

For all the difficulties there are in getting at roe does, particularly in the depths of winter, the wariness of that beautiful species does not hold a candle to fallow deer does. These difficult deer were not present in any numbers on Bourn Valley Farms but were prolific on Eve. I have described above how I tackled the business of shooting male fallow deer and put the most effort into this part of my assignment during August and September. After a year or two, the cull returns demonstrated I was delivering a male fallow deer cull in accordance with my planned target. I wished I could say the same about the fallow doe cull, but could not claim to be achieving anything like the numbers wanted. There were obvious reasons for this. The fallow does were hefted to the sanctuary off but immediately adjacent to Eve's land. In the winter the short, dangerous for deer day light hours meant the fallow does could sit these out in the safety and security of the sanctuary and then step over the boundary on to Eve after dark, returning the same way before day light. On many occasions I observed these does on the sanctuary paddocks watching the adjacent fields and woods belonging to Eve, and perhaps also even watching me. They had a habit of lining up and looking into Eve's ground over the paddock railings of the sanctuary, whilst waiting for darkness to fall. That was frustrating for me and taught me that I was dealing with a superior, sharp quarry that was going to be much more difficult to grass than some inexperienced, brainless pricket out for a romp in my fields. Although there were to be exceptions, the majority of fallow does that visited Eve were in and out during the hours of darkness and, if on Eve's ground at all during daylight hours, were as sharp as razors. Devising productive strategies for the undoing of these unbelievably wary deer was to preoccupy my winter months throughout the following years.

There was a wood on Eve separated from the sanctuary by just one field. This was a triangular shaped wood with the base of the triangle being at the bottom of a slope. A small stream ran from left to right just inside the wood and outside the land rose again to a track, hedge and ditch that overlooked the bottom of the wood. By standing in the ditch, with my head and shoulders through a hole I had cut in the bottom of the hedge, I had a discreet view of perhaps two hundred and fifty yards of the woodland edge. This was useful as the local fallow deer favoured a route along the outside of the wood.

On the first morning I decided to try this spot, I arrived very early so that I could walk into my hide under the cover of darkness. Approaching the spot from the field at the back of it, I dropped into the ditch and settled so that, with the arrival of the light, I would be able to sweep my binoculars over the bottom edge of the wood that was in front of me. The light was not long coming, with the blackness of the early hours being gradually replaced by first a subfusc and then a grey hue. As I deployed the binoculars the shapes of the trees in the wood became more readily identifiable and other features such as tree stumps became clearer.

As one does in the pre-shooting light, I made out the first deer- a doe and calf- as deer shapes within the wood and could only confirm them as deer when they moved. I watched and waited, and my predominant feeling was that I would not see deer outside the wood, and that I was wasting my time by sitting in a ditch by a track that was also a public footpath and, very shortly, would be heavily walked by the public. I lacked confidence in my own plan and was close to giving it up when three fallow does came from the left. They gave all the appearance of being trekkers as they walked along the outside of the wood and into my killing zone less than one hundred yards in front of me. A sharp whistle held them up and I nailed the middle beast, because she happened to pause just right for a shot. I heard the thwack of the bullet in her lungs and watched her turn into the shot and run towards me before collapsing. She had been dead on her feet.

At that time I had no quad bike for the extraction of beasts, so suffered a sharp drag of the doe over the sticky soil in the field and to the track. Then, with confidence in my strategy now sky high, I took the fallow doe back to the larder in the back of my truck. With a favourable wind, I was able to repeat this ambush with success several times that first season at Eve. The natural camouflage of my hide, the steady rest provided by my short bipod on the verge of the track and the wide fields of view and fire were all factors in it's continuing success that winter. Above all else, however, the deer path along the outside of the wood supplied a steady supply of fallow deer does for me to engage. At the end of February I was keenly looking forward to replicating the ambush strategy there when the fallow doe season came round again, having every confidence the does would continue to go this way. It was not to be. In March a contract forestry team came into the bottom of the wood and erected a deer fence to facilitate the regeneration of coppice stools in the compartment. That fence caused the local fallow deer to use different routes and paths and what had, only a few months before, been a busy deerway was reduced to a mere by-way.

The biggest wood on Eve was just over fifty acres. It was more or less square and had several quite different compartments in it. These included a compartment of fir trees, a derelict and near impenetrable stand of wind blown trees, hazel coppice in various stages of regeneration and a couple of thickets not long coppiced with supplementary replanting. There were also some compartments predominantly comprising standards. Some of these compartments were divided by rides. This wood and those adjoining it provided sufficient cover to house a fairly permanent population of fallow deer. Prior to the rut there would be several does in Fifty Wood, which I would see when I was in there culling muntjac in the summer months. I enjoyed the charming cameos I had whilst watching the does with their progeny grazing on the summer evening rides. Then, the bucks would come in for the rut and disturb the peace. Fifty Wood in particular usually had a magnificent resident stand buck and for a few days it was like a cattle market in there. Then, as the rut fizzled out in the last week of October, the bucks went and invariably took the does with them. So it was that by the opening of the doe season on the 1st. November fallow does were disappearing out of Fifty Wood and the adjoining coverts on Eve like water down a drain.

However, not all the fallow does departed and I tackled those that stayed. Fifty Wood was flat, and surrounded by well walked footpaths. The walkers did not all stay on the paths; the more brazen ones entered and walked in the wood, using the mown rides. I concluded that it would be bad practice to shoot from the ground in this location. However, I had erected high seats for shooting muntjac, and felt that these, when moved to overlook deer paths, would provide safe sure shooting platforms for fallow deer culling. After some false starts, I placed two seats to cover major rides one being for use in the prevailing south westerly wind whilst the other suited a wind from the north or east. These seats being inside the wood, I could never sit in them and be wholly right for wind. Almost inevitably, my scent would be winding some part of the wood so my practice was to consider before going anywhere near either high seat, which compartments I would wind and whether these were critical.

Other aspects I was conscious of were the near dormancy of fallow does during the cold winter days, their reluctance to get out of their bedding areas and their consequent failure to present me with shooting chances. I resolved to change their behaviour by supplying feedstuffs and minerals. This involved me in obtaining and dropping lumps of rock salt on the rides and feeding bags of windfall apples, carrots, milling barley and any other feed that I could obtain. This I found was an effective tactic after Christmas, when natural food supplies were scarce.

An immediate bonus of having the feed and mineral blocks on the ride was the confidence it gave me to stay in my high seat on cold winter mornings. Looking at a pile of apples surrounded by footings, I would tell myself that I really fancied my chances of catching out a doe returning to them for another feed.

I remember one December morning on which I got myself in to Fifty Wood in good time for the morning session. In other words, I was in the seat and settled well before it was light. There were a heap of apples front left of me at about sixty yards distance from my perch. Dawn is never warm at that time of year and I shivered in the seat and waited impatiently for the coming of the light. As it came and reached a point at which although still insufficient to shoot by or make out objects clearly, it was possible to see shapes I saw a small deer shape on the ride in front... a muntjac by the look of it. I would have passed on that so early in the stalk even if there had been sufficient light in which to shoot. Next, there was a movement in the middle of the ride. I couldn't see what had caused it with my naked eye but a sweep with my binoculars enabled me to identify a woodcock. I watched it, fascinated, in spite of the cold. It was feeding, finding worms under the wet grass. A cock pheasant appeared at the furthest end of the ride and, in crossing from one side to the other, disappeared into the coppiced hazels.

I shivered again. All this nature study was interesting enough, but I had a job to do, a cull to achieve. It's so easy to lose confidence in a high seat on a cold December morning. As I sat there losing it, and feeling very tempted to get down and take a prowl round the wood, I tried to redress my morale. I knew there were usually fallow deer in Fifty Wood; it was inconceivable that there were none that morning. The wind was as good for the high seat as it could ever be. Whilst possible that beasts approaching from my back right would wind me this was not the way I expected then to come. The apple feed was, I knew, being used, and food elsewhere in the wood and on the farm was in short supply. I tried to convince myself that the fallow would come to the apples, and that all I needed to do was to sit tight and wait until that happened.

Pre-occupied with these mind games, I looked round again and suddenly became aware that daylight had come. The light had improved as if in a minute and the shapes on the ride edges and in the wood itself were changed; no longer indistinct, each one was identifiable. Now, in my high seat, with the absence of leaves on the winter trees, I felt visible. I at once gave up the idea of getting down and going still hunting; it was too late for that now. I would never get near the crafty does. All I could do was wait.

Conscious of my presence in the middle of the wood, I practised sitting still as never before. I sat there as if comatose. My eyes swivelled as I observed the scene, but my head stayed still. I had a small flask in my bag and wanted a hot drink but I left it there. My rifle rested on the shooting rails round the seat, ready for me to shoulder with minimum movement.

Eight o'clock had long gone that morning and in truth it was nearer nine when a watery sun broke through the gloom. It's thin rays shone on the ride to my left and revived my enthusiasm. I thought there was surely a chance the fallow would move now. I visualised the grey winter coated does becoming impatient to vacate the bedding areas, wanting the sun's warmth on their backs and my apples in their stomachs. I waited and the sun warmed me a little bit too. Ten minutes later, my swivelling eye was stopped by the sight of a fallow doe's head on the left hand side of the ride. All I could see was her head, fifty yards to my left. The ride was slightly raised in the middle and the edges of it were a foot or two lower. The doe, still screened by the cover, appeared to be looking up at me and observing me. All I could do was stay still and I did. I sat so still my neck started to hurt, but I did not move. The doe's head was immovable too.

Then, in one fluid movement, she was on the ride. She was a fine sight in the early morning sun, with the glint of rain drops on her coat and the hint of steam from her hot breath. Standing there, at once alert and relaxed, she was living proof that every doe looks far more beautiful alive than she does dead. With all the difficulties I had in getting to grips with my fallow does, this was a tense moment for me. I made myself shoulder the rifle so slowly that I feared she would walk away whilst I did so, but was conscious it would be fatal to reveal myself by rushing. Even so, she got me as the rifle came up to my shoulder, and her head was alert and raised when the bullet ended the business. My shot echoed round the ride, and another fallow doe was destined for a hook in the chiller.

The sun is the winter stalker's friend and I found out that it's profitable to pay close attention to the wood faces, hedges and banks on which it is shining. One morning I was stalking Twenty Wood on Eve. I had a young friend with me as an observer, and with the added difficulty of still hunting in the company of an inexperienced follower I elected to sit up in a two seater high seat that overlooked the deer lawn in the middle of the wood. There was a sharp frost that morning and the grass on the deer lawn was white with it. My friend and I sat up and never saw so much as an ear, although at that time the deer lawn was a spot greatly favoured by the local fallow deer. At length, with the sun coming up and shining into the top end of Twenty Wood, and with my seat and the deer lawn remaining white with frost and still in bone cold shade, I sent my shivering friend off on a circular walk that would take him round the top of the wood and back to me at the seat. I knew this would warm him up and hoped against hope he might move any deer in the top of the wood my way. Half an hour later he reappeared in a state of great excitement. He related that having followed the route I had given him he had arrived at a point which enabled him to look at the top of Twenty Wood, which was bathed in sunshine. There, he said, he had seen more than thirty fallow deer standing about in the sunshine. He told me he had watched them for some while and that, when he approached them, they were reluctant to move off, as if they were enjoying that sunny spot so much. As I descended the high seat, bone cold and shivering, my sympathies were all with the deer.

Since then, on a cold, frosty outing for fallow does, I search out wood faces and other places which will be in full sun at whatever time of day it is that I am taking an outing. It's easily said that the low ground deer stalker should station himself where the sun is shining, but on flat ground this will likely involve having sufficient high seats to cover different wood faces as the sun moves round.

I was stalking with a young soldier friend during another bitterly cold spell. At the start of it there had been fall of snow followed by freezing conditions, since when the frost had been in the ground for days. In places, it was impossible to stalk silently because the noise underfoot from the frozen snow. All ponds and puddles were frozen up and the landscape was rimed in white. Every blade of drilled wheat was a short white frozen spear and the branches of the trees on the woodland edges were all frosted. It was most inhospitable and really unsuitable for sitting around, with temperatures down to minus ten or twelve, and ordinarily I might not have gone out. However, young "Army" had only limited leave so we met in the yard before dawn with our very breath condensing in the frozen air as we breathed. We split up, one in Fifty Wood and the other on another woodland edge. Neither of us saw so much as an ear, and returned to the yard well chilled shortly before 9a.m. As the light came, it was accompanied by a form of freezing fog, which had prevented the sun breaking though. Throughout our time on the ground it had stayed freezing cold. We spent the morning attending to some of the chores that are incidental to practical deer management and went for an early lunch in the local pub. Whilst we were at lunch, the sun broke though the fog and the day became, as if by magic, almost alpine. The sky was clear and blue and the sun shone full on the south and south west woodland edges. As we went out to stalk again on what we knew would be a short December afternoon, we were surprised to see large numbers of deer on the wood's edge with others actually out in the fields. These were fallow deer, and so congenitally crepuscular that they were generally only ever seen in the hours immediately either side of dawn and dusk.

On that particular afternoon, the ambush that Army and I had planned was wrecked by the fallow having come out on the top of the day before we were in position . The herd was out in force and, with the noise every footstep in the snow made, there was not a cat in hell's chance of getting into them. The next day, I had a lie-in and drove over to the stalking ground in the late morning. The sun was trying to break through as I essayed a discreet route into my high seat. Although I made it without, as far as I know, disturbing any beasts, it was a good thing I wasn't any later. Within a few minutes the scene was sun drenched and, as I enjoyed the warmth of it on my face and chest, deer popped out of the woods here there and everywhere. I looked at my watch. It was 1330 hrs and the number of animals all around me made the frozen farm look like a deer park. I had never previously seen undisturbed deer out in the open in numbers such as these.

The outcome of this mid-day visit was that I culled a fallow doe and calf. At the start of my unique, personal "deer everywhere moment", I had been frustrated by my ability to do anything about them. With the ground so bare of cover after prolonged snow and frost and the bright winter sun providing the clearest visibility there was no chance of my moving at all, no way of my getting at any of the deer. I had to stay where I was, observing and waiting in the hope that a cull beast would venture within range. Eventually, my patience was rewarded in this way. A doe and calf, which had been well out- several hundred yards away – from the woodland where I was, showed themselves and, after some dithering, started to come back towards me. It was as if the doe had suddenly become uneasy about being exposed in the open in the middle of the day, and she was visibly anxious to regain the shelter and cover of the wood. She brought the calf back on a route that was likely to bring her directly under my high seat and so, before she came too close, I had to stop her with a shout. She heard the shout and paused not broadside but with enough angle for me to see and shoot just behind the left foreleg. She went down and the calf ran a few yards and then stopped and looked back, so I was able to dispatch that too. It turned out she was a doe calf too.

As I retrieved the carcasses from the now otherwise deserted field, I didn't feel very comfortable with myself for putting pressure on the deer during such extreme conditions. It seemed unfair to be adding to their difficulties. The subsequent session in the deer larder diminished such scruples. Both beasts were in superb condition, with abundant fat stores and full stomachs. These deer were thriving, and as I had just seen with my own eyes, there were many more of them. Since that day, I have spied the field on which I culled those two fallow deer and the adjacent fields on numerous occasions and have rarely seen a beast at all other than at the beginning and end of the day. However, I am now ready for the temperature to fall below freezing and the frost and snow to set in. When this happens, it is ingrained in me to take a flask and rug and sit up in the winter sunshine on the top of the day. These sun bathing deer were and are a reminder that deer do not operate by the clock as we do, but respond to and exploit the conditions and try to survive as best they can, however cold it is.

Experiences such as these with fallow does also made me more open minded about the time for ending deer stalking outings. Formerly, if I agreed a rendezvous with a guest stalker, I would expect it to be kept. After gaining more understanding of how even a small shift in the wind or the coming into sun of a place could result in deer appearing there I became more tolerant and flexible. On occasion, it might be myself who needed more time to make a cull; on others it would be my guest. Towards the top of Twenty Wood, there was a point beyond which the wood line angled inwards. This location was thereby sheltered from the prevailing wind and, on a windy day, was distinctly more comfortable and calm. I was able to erect a high seat overlooking this and was stunned by the number and variety of birds and animals that used it. Sometimes where the wood edge was exposed to the wind there would not be a living thing. At the same time, the sheltered zone would be alive with wild life.

I waited in my high seat overlooking this on many evenings. On one that I remember well, the light ebbed away as I sat there making sweep after fruitless sweep with my binoculars. I had almost given up hope of getting a shot when I became aware of a pale, nearly white, shape on the woodland edge. It was a fallow doe, which had just bobbed down and up the ditch to emerge on the grass outside. I could see her through the binoculars, but it was possibly too dark to see her through the rifle scope. I raised the rifle and at first saw a blurred pale shape. I couldn't see enough of her clearly enough to engage her. I screwed down the magnification, and as I did, became aware she had moved a few yards towards me, out of the shadow of the wood. A shot was on, and eschewing any heroics, I aimed for the top of her heart. The recoil from the shot blinded me to the result and I was only aware of the shapes of deer in the near darkness vacating the field.

Getting down, I put on my head torch and walked across the field to the place I judged my cull beast had been standing. I couldn't see anything : no blood or hair. There was no sign she had ever stood there. I walked to the wood and looked in the ditch. There was nothing there. That was a disappointment as a stricken doe will often run in her death flight to a ditch and drop in it. Choosing the most heavily used of several deer paths that went into the wood, I shone my torch around the woodland floor, fortunately fairly sparsely covered there. And then I got lucky. The light coloured doe was lying ten yards inside the wood on the line I would have expected. I approached her cautiously, but it was all over for her. That beast went to the deer larder like many others, but in my memory bank she became tagged as another doe extracted from that sheltered spot.

If I have given the impression that my encounters with fallow deer does were generally successful then it is a misleading one. I have, rather, highlighted some successful stalks which remain fresh in the mind, in several cases, years later just because fruitful outings against the does were so few and far between. At times in the winter, the woods on Eve seemed to be devoid of deer and I would likely go for several outings without seeing one. It was hard to keep at it then and a look at the next day's weather forecast in December and January would often predict rain, storms, sleet, snow or frost, or sometimes several of these, which were off putting. I found the best motivation then was to have a committed companion to take out, one who would be genuinely disappointed if his outing was cancelled. Even so, six or seven blank outings in a row sometimes made me think there was easier sport to be had in East Anglia than stalking fallow deer does.

Chapter Thirteen

My Deer Dogs

BEFORE TAKING TO deerstalking, I had always kept one or two working gun dogs at home, either labradors or springer spaniels or, sometimes, both of these breeds. Few of these dogs had paper pedigrees. What they all had in common were working backgrounds and, such was my enthusiasm for all forms of shooting, they had plenty of work. At that time, I favoured hard going dogs capable of undertaking a full day's work and giving one hundred and twenty five percent commitment. Having had such wonderful times with my dogs in the shooting field I was concerned how, if at all, they would fit into my new pursuit of low ground deerstalking.

From my reading of books on deerstalking, I realised that dogs were not only a useful but an essential asset for the deerstalker in his pursuit. I read about the training and use of dogs in continental Europe and the way in which deer stalkers there favoured robust breeds such as wire haired pointers, vizlas and Bavarian mountain hounds for deer work and also rough haired teckels. I gleaned from these accounts some theoretical knowledge of deer tracking and how to approach the task of finding lost dead or wounded deer. I was uncertain as to how much of this would be relevant to my conditions in lowland England on ground were there were muntjac, but no boar, and were deer driving would not be practised as such.

As, at that time, I already owned two gundogs – one springer and one Labrador- I baulked at buying a specialist deer dog. I decided to try out my Labrador. I gave him a dry run early on by dragging a freshly shot roe buck across a grass area. The buck was bleeding heavily and left a heavy blood trail. I hid the buck's carcase in the grass at the end of the trail and brought back Bison, my labrador, on a long lead. As we reached the point at which the buck had been shot, he lunged forward in an excited way, and surged along the blood trail nearly pulling my arm off in the process. He led me straight to the concealed buck and surprised me by making something of a demonstration over it, growling and worrying it. He was normally a good natured old dog and so I felt with his reactions to this deer carcass that I was seeing another side of him. I also judged that on the basis of the false trail trial Bison would likely find me a lost deer. I decided to take him with me when I went stalking and that I would leave him in my truck during the stalking outing. He would then be there all ready and "on call" so to speak should he be needed.

I was soon to find that the books were right and that it was essential to have a dog for the purposes of low ground stalking. When I was stalking roe bucks in high summer, I found it extraordinary how well shot bucks could be lost in crop or natural cover. It was almost unbelievable that a buck in summer coat, that seemed such a large animal, could vanish without trace in almost any vegetation. One morning, I shot a roe buck on the edge of the reed bed at Bourn. The buck lunged immediately on being shot and ran into the reeds, which closed behind it as if it had never been there. Fearful of messing up any blood trail, I didn't even attempt to find that buck myself but went back to the truck for Bison. The old fellow seemed to have remembered his dry run as he pulled on the lead all the way to the reed bed. As before, I had him start at the point where the buck had been shot and commanded him to "Find the buck!". He just put his old head down and made for the reeds with myself hanging on to his lead at least until we reached them. At that point, I lost hold of the lead and heard Bison crashing through the reeds on his own and ahead of me. It was high summer and the reeds were well over my head and I couldn't see deer or dog. I stopped and listened and then heard Bison growling off to my right. Making my way through the reeds I found him worrying the carcass of the buck, which must have headed that way in it's final flight, after entering the swamp in a way which suggested he would travel across it in a straight line.

The distance the buck had travelled in its death flight was no more than fifty yards but my chances of finding it in that cover would have been slim, particularly as he had turned nearly ninety degrees once inside the reed bed and gone in an unexpected direction. I dragged him out into the open in triumphant mood. I felt a double satisfaction: My shot had found the bottom of the heart, and my dog had recovered the beast.

I remember Bison recovering another roe deer for me. I had shot this in dirty ground, in an area which had formerly been a quarry and was full of hillocks and hollows, drains and gutters. My shot had been a long one and in fading light. By the time I got Bison to the spot where I judged the deer had been standing the last of the light had drained out of the sky and I was unable to pinpoint the place. Without much hope, and without even being certain about the outcome of the shot, I cast off Bison and stood still listening to him crash through the considerable amount of summer undergrowth. Happily for me, these sounds ceased and were replaced by Bison's"deer found" dog vocal. I went over to the gutter from which the growling was emanating and found him standing on top of the roe deer that had obviously collapsed head first into it.

A distinctive feature of my muntjac stalking, particularly on the Eve Estate, was that many of the muntjac were accounted for from high seats within the woods. With a rolling forestry programme on the Estate the best seats were often positioned on the edge of compartments that comprised thickets of coppice regrowth with large drifts of near impenetrable bramble. Each of these was of course it's own muntjac city! The preferred shot, particularly when the muntjac was on the edge of the thicket, was a touch forward, through either the shoulders or the neck. This shot would put the muntjac straight down where it stood, and would not affect it's value for the dealer or the table, as it left the haunches and saddle undamaged. However, the muntjac were not always co-operative and, being such busy restless little deer, often declined to present for the perfect shot.

I learnt early on that any other shots than those described would be likely to result in the stricken muntjac bolting back into the thicket and being the very devil to find. The first occasion this happened was to be a bench mark for this as my guest for the morning was armed

105

with no less a rifle than a .270 with, I think, 130 grain bullets. Before first light on a September morning I left him in a promising high seat in Fifty Wood. My friend was an experienced red deer stalker so I left him there with instructions to stay put until I collected him at the end of the session. I went off to stalk another wood and, whilst so doing, was pleased to hear two shots with an interval of half an hour between them. I forget whether I was successful that morning or not but when I returned to my friend, he climbed down from the high seat and told me that he had shot a fallow pricket shortly after the light came and, later, a muntjac buck. We walked up the ride and the fallow pricket lay on one side of it, having dropped within a yard or two from where it was shot. The muntjac was nowhere to be seen although my friend was adamant that he had, as he put it, knocked it off it's feet. After a short, fruitless search off the edge of the ride, I decided to call on Bison's services. This was the first muntjac I had asked him to find but I had no reason to suppose he would treat it any differently from a roe deer trail. He started in off the ride, straight away disappearing into the bramble bushes and I was able to follow his progress from the shaking movement made by these. He went in a semi circle and then seemed to stop. As there was no chance of my getting through the brambles I had to run up the ride and find a way into the thicket further along. Then using my stalking stick to bash down the worst of them I reached Bison in the back of the patch where he was worrying the dead deer. A few minutes later, scratched but happy, I was able to present my friend with his first muntjac buck. I was chuffed to bits by Bison's effort on that beast and by the recovery of a carcass that would have been lost without him. If ever there was a find that convinced me of the necessity for a deer dog then this was it.

Since then Bison and his successors have spent many hours snoozing in the back of my truck whilst I have been stalking. They have become used to that routine and have usually been found by myself to be fast asleep on my return from the fields and woods. My dogs have not usually been required on my deer stalking outings. Low ground deer stalking being what it is, many of these have been blank. When I or my associates have had shots, the targeted deer has usually been readily recovered by the deerstalker without recourse to a dog. When our deer have run into thick cover it's been a different story and a search with a dog has been required and has more often than not result in the lost beast being found.

One morning I was culling fallow as a guest of a kind friend of mine and was positioned for the morning session in a fine high seat overlooking fifteen or more acres of rough, tall pampas grass, in which had been planted a variety of young hardwoods, each of which was contained in it's own tree guard. It was evidently a place favoured by the resident fallow deer and, after watching much of interest, I was lucky enough to engage a flat top fallow pricket. I use the word "lucky" advisedly because the combination of grass fronds, tree guards and tree branches meant it was necessary to thread the bullet round these features to avoid the disappointment of a missed or, much worse, a wounded beast. The main characteristic needed by the stalker here was that of patience and, when I finally took a shot, I believed it was with the benefit of a clear line of fire. I was therefore worried when my quarry made off without any reaction to the shot at all.

My fiend had instructed me to await his return before leaving the high seat and so I spent some fraught time until he came for me. I explained what had happened and took him into the grass to the point at which I thought the deer had been standing. Once there, I became alarmed by the amount of cover such as fallen branches, brambles and the like that might have obstructed or deflected my bullet. I now thought that the deer might have been standing behind one particularly big branch that I had not seen at all. Even more disturbing was the complete absence of any sign. There was no paint or pins to be seen anywhere. I stood there, and I feel sure many low ground deerstalkers will recognise my emotions, which were miserable and distressed. I was up to my waist in acres of rough grass and young whips without the slightest clue as to the whereabouts of my beast, or even whether it was dead, wounded or missed and gone away. I am sure I visualised the worst case scenario.

We stood there flummoxed until my friend sensibly enquired whether I would like to get my dog, which he knew was in the truck. He waited there, marking the spot without compromising the scent until I returned with my spaniel, Brandy, another old timer now in a long succession of working gun dogs. Brought up on pheasants, Brandy is not much interested in deer but will seek and find one when I ask him, if it is there to be found. That morning, he hunted the area I indicated, much of the time out of sight in the grasses. Then, as he worked further away from me, I sensed he had stopped, followed him as best I could and found him licking the blood from the exit wound on the right hand side of the pricket's chest. I was relieved and delighted to have found the beast. My friend was appreciative of the dog's tidy exhibition and scenting ability. Not for the first time, I was conscious of that roller coaster of adrenalin that not infrequently follows the deerstalker's shot: the disappearance of the beast into cover and then it's subsequent recovery.

When, in a "deer lost!" situation, a dead deer is retrieved from cover then this is, as I have shown, a cause for satisfaction. This is never more so than on a summer or autumn evening when a carcass left out ungralloched overnight will likely be spoiled and unfit to eat. However, the recovery of a wounded deer puts the work of the dog concerned into a higher league. The unfortunate beast may have been injured in a road traffic accident, by rogue dogs or by a bullet from a rifle or pellets from a poacher's shot gun. Whatever the cause- be it legal or lawless- the outcome for the deer will likely be bleak and I am absolutely certain that the keeping of a dog for deer increases the deerstalker's chances of rescuing bad situations and bringing them to as satisfactory a conclusion as can be achieved.

An experience I had one early autumn evening illustrates why I hold such a strong view on this. I went out to stalk the far end of Peninsular Farm, where the land tapers to a point. At that end, I could shoot from one side to the other and had the benefit of a bank which I could use as a safe backstop. On that particular evening I had with me my son's little sprocker bitch, Lark, who, whilst primarily a small game shooting dog, has a natural instinct both for stalking and for finding shot deer. As my route that evening was to be along the edge of a field in stubble, and possibly also a ditch overgrown with nettles, I left the bitch in my truck and set off for a cautious stalk. The land I was stalking comprised two fields in wheat stubble, in the shape of an arrowhead and I was stalking towards the point of it. There was the nettle filled ditch on my side, another ditch through the middle and a third ditch (with the bank on the far side of it) on the far side. There was a confluence of these three watercourses at the point of the arrow. On top of the bank there was a thick hedge and immediately the other side of that a thick, head high mixed soghum and maize game cover.

As I approached the point where I intended to wait in ambush for an hour or so I became aware of a roe buck lying undisturbed on the edge of the stubble under the bank. He was on my ground and by dropping into the nettled ditch beside me I was able to make enough ground to gain a firing position from which I could take a safe shot. I settled myself on the brew of the ditch, with my rifle resting on a bipod and waited for the buck to stand. When it did, I engaged it with an engine room shot and floored him where he stood. I must say I was not happy about the outcome of the shot as the buck kicked and wriggled for some time in a manner that suggested his spine had been creased. I waited and waited until he was still and then waited some more. Finally, I walked over towards him and, as I approached, and to my horror, he was up and away into the game cover before I could take another shot. Being well aware of the length and thickness of that particular cover I must say I thought the prospects of ever finding that beast were negligible and that my one and only chance was to put Lark to work.

I took her to the spot where the buck had fallen and lain for so long and there was plenty of blood there from which she could start her hunt. She sniffed it and jumped over the ditch, through the hedge and up the bank and into the cover crop at speed. Almost immediately, I heard the noise of a bigger animal in the crop and then a minute or two later the bark of a deer from what seemed to be the far end of the game strip. I couldn't see anything so ran down to that end of the strip where there was a hedge and grass strip going left handed towards the edge of a big wood.

As I arrived there, I saw a roe buck running back towards me from about one hundred yards distance and he was being closely pursued and worried by the sprocker. The exhausted buck, half falling and half throwing itself down with Lark leaping on top of him, was almost at my feet and I had a few anxious moments before I could take a clear close range shot to his head and dispatch him. What I found when I examined him amazed me. Lark had plainly tackled him with ferocity as one of his testicles was missing and the other was attached to him by a thread six inches below his groin. This little dog, whose evenings would happily be spent on the lap of any member of my family prepared to pet her, had shown me a whole new side to her character. She had tracked that roe buck into cover, chased it a hundred yards through the cover and another hundred yards along the grass strip. She had then coursed it back, driven it down at my feet. At some point she had attacked and emasculated it and, assuming she was thrown off had carried on the hunt with real determination and courage. Her's was a stunning effort which had got me out of a bad mess. Forever after it, I was aware that within this lovely, soft, gentle natured lapdog there lingered a she wolf. I never underestimated her again. For the record, my bullet had found what a forestry stalker of my acquaintance calls the blind spot. With the deer standing broadside, it had passed through the narrow space between the top of the lungs and the spine.

Another illustrative incident of this nature involved my friend Jack and his labrador Smoker. At the date of it Smoker would have been six or seven years old, a tall, strong, rangy dog with an independent no nonsense character. He had no time for anyone except Jack and the two of them habitually stalked together with Smoker invariably accompanying Jack throughout the whole process. However long and hard the day's sport was, Smoker would put his parts on at the end of the day by lying down and refusing to get into the truck for the journey home. His inference was that the day or outing had not been commensurate with his notion of a day's sport and, even after many outings rough shooting and stalking I never saw him concede this point and admit he had had enough. In all, Smoker was a great character. With Jack being a good shot, and low ground deer stalking being the pursuit it is, I never had occasion to see Smoker in action as a deer dog although I understood that after one bad, painful experience he habitually held muntjac by the back of the neck and all other deer species by the throat.

On this particular evening, Jack was stalking with Smoker on the edge of Fifty Wood when they spotted fallow deer grazing the drilled wheat on the west side of the wood. There was the chance of a safe shot so Jack stalked to the wood edge and, with the parcel of fallow deer becoming alarmed and preparing to make off, hurriedly engaged a doe that ran back into the wood obviously injured. Jack sent Smoker and in the space of a few seconds he had leapt on the doe and was holding it down by the throat, which enabled Jack to finish the business. That night Smoker had earned the treat of deer's heart he was habitually given after a successful stalk.

I had a lot of time for Smoker not least because his reaction to once being slashed by a muntjac was to seize it by a different hold and so avoid being wounded again by it's canine teeth. Neither he or his master considered he should be retired from muntjac retrieving by reason of his war wound and it was smart of the dog to adapt his line of attack for that species and to make a distinction between muntjac and roe. After all, the two species would not be so dissimilar in size and appearance to a dog.

On another occasion, a friend of mine was stalking with me as my guest at Bourn Valley Farms when he put down a roe buck down to a shot off his sticks. The beast then jumped up again and made off at speed up a hill and away through two fields of standing wheat. My own dogs made nothing of the scent and the faintest of blood trails, which comprised occasional small spots of blood on the wheat leaves. After their failure, I called out some friends for an impromptu drive, expecting to find the buck lying up in the rough beyond the boundary of the second field. We never saw him. In despair, I called out a friend, a professional stalker, with an experienced teckel in the hope that he would track the injured deer. In what was by then the late evening, the teckel did no better than my gun dogs. A week later, I stalked the same buck and shot him whilst he was running a doe. He had an open and bloody injury from the cut skin at the front of his throat. Whilst the shock of the bullet's passage had no doubt temporarily interrupted the blood supply and caused the knock down, it had not been sufficiently serious to affect his sex life.

My experience has been that the value of a dog in low ground deer stalking is in it's finding ability and I believe my dual purpose gun dogs have performed well in that department. I have never greatly rated the assistance a dog gives the deer stalker by indicating unshot deer in cover. I had a diminutive spaniel bitch at one time and she would point deer in cover, which I could not see. I had a Labrador that would snuffle alarmingly loudly in the same circumstances. The trouble was none of these dogs could bring the deer out into the open where I could engage them. Against the theoretical advantage of having a dog that would indicate uninjured deer was the disadvantage of stalking in the company of a dog that would not necessarily freeze when I froze or keep perfectly still for hours at a time under my high seat. On balance, although I enjoyed the company of a dog out stalking, my opinion was that it was best left in the truck until after the shot had been taken and, if at all, it was needed for a search. This particularly applied in the winter time when the cover was sparse. My friend Jack disagreed with me and he and Smoker shared some good times together. Once in a blue moon Smoker, being on the spot, rescued his master by pulling down and holding an injured beast and Jack valued this more than the occasional loss of a chance when Smoker moved at the wrong moment and spooked the deer.

Having a parallel interest in game and rough shooting, I have had a continuing need for gun dogs, particularly springer spaniels. My spaniels and Labradors have all found deer as well as flushing and retrieving game birds, rabbits and hares. As they have carried out these tasks in a reasonably efficient way I have never had a specialist continental breed of deer dog. No doubt in extreme circumstances, I could have done with a big, bold wirehaired or one of his ilk but, on the whole, I have been well served by a succession of labradors and spaniels, that have picked up the tasks required of them as dogs for deer in addition to their roles as rough and game shooting dogs. As is illustrated by my account of the recovery by Lark of the Peninsular Farm roe buck, the instinct of a working dog against deer is inherent and inbred.

Having had and used my gun dogs for my low ground deerstalking activities has given me much pleasure. In fact, my gun dogs have been an integral part of my life and I would not go shooting or stalking without them. Over the years, I have had to take account of the needs and housing of my gun dogs when, for example, I have wanted to go away on holiday. I have spent a lot of money on buying and maintaining my gun dogs and on veterinary bills when they have been ill or injured. I grudge neither the lifestyle impact or the money spent on my dogs because I owe so much to them both as a shooting man and a deerstalker. To adapt a famous quote, I would say of the most fun I have had in life, "I owe it to rifle, dog and gun."

Sadly, I seem to be in a minority over this. In a line of game shooting guns, I not uncommonly notice that mine is the only gun dog. Enquiries of the other guns as to where their dogs are typically reveal that they have a rug rat in London or travel abroad a lot, or that "their daughter has asthma". No doubt these are all valid excuses but they are unhelpful when the moment comes that a winged cock pheasant is running down a ditch, and the shoot pickers up are all busy at the other end of the line. Many deerstalkers are just as bad and few of the many guests I have hosted have a deer dog or any working dog at all. These characters rely on others to recover a deer down and lost in cover or, worse still, a wounded deer.

The attitude I admire is that of one good friend who was a consumate deerstalker. . Although living in a town, he was invariably accompanied by one of his favourite teckels. Whilst his shooting was so straight that he rarely needed the services of his dog it is indicative of his good attitude that he had one there for the assistance of his, often less accurate, associates. I know for sure that his teckels found deer for them that would otherwise have been lost on several occasions.

Another good friend of mine, a worthy man who has done a great deal for field sports, marked his retirement by acquiring a Bavarian Mountain Hound bitch. Possessive to a fault around the home, she is mustard at tracking a blood trail and, still a youngster, has already proved her worth by finding beasts at last light that would have spoiled if left out overnight. I admire my friend's enterprise in trying such a specialist dog and applaud the commitment to his low ground deerstalking that this implies. Were the German requirement that every deer stalker has access to a dog trained to track deer imposed here one wonders how many low ground deerstalkers, without either their own dogs or access to the dogs of others, would have to hang up their rifles or, perhaps, take up target shooting.

Chapter Fourteen

Guest Stalkers

RATHER LIKE THE distinction made in the Highlands of Scotland between the deerstalker – the professional stalker- and the rifle- the amateur guest stalker. This aptly reflects the deerstalker's role in managing the day and stalking the deer and the guest's responsibility for the shot. In hill stalking there is a well established convention or etiquette in the conduct of the day which is, for example, illustrated by the stalker leading and the rifle following in his footsteps on the hill. Such practices were plainly established many years ago when the sport of deer stalking on the open hill was in it's infancy. Unfortunately, low ground stalking lacks that long pedigree and there is less established acceptance as to how it should be conducted. The stalking also takes place in different circumstances and, when undertaken in woodland, with different reactions being required of the rifle. As my interest in deer stalking has been for my own personal enjoyment, and not for gain, I have never taken out clients. However, over the years I have enjoyed being host to numerous guests on my various stalking grounds.

My attitude to guests is that if they are unfamiliar with my ground then they must be restricted to high seat stalking, even though they may be experienced deerstalkers, unless I am to act as their deerstalker and take them out under my supervision. If they are to be in a high seat, I brief each of them personally as to any dangers there may be in shooting in certain directions or distances from that seat. If a visiting deerstalker has been on that part of my ground before sufficiently often to recognise the hazards and the boundaries, then I may allocate a route for him to follow with, perhaps, one or two high seats to visit. I debrief him at the end of the stalk to ascertain whether he has followed instructions. These arrangements have served me well and safely over the years. Although it may sound boring for a visiting rifle to be restricted to one high seat many of my own outings comprise just that, particularly my winter outings after fallow deer when still hunting through the woods and fields becomes particularly difficult and unproductive.

The characteristics and quirks of the guest rifles, whom I have hosted for such outings have given me much amusement over the years. Just occasionally, these have also been the cause of no little anger on my part.

I recall as my best guests those old hands happy to watch deer by the hour and bide their time for a shot. When and if that moment comes they can conclude the business with a clinical rifle bullet in the bottom half of the heart. Their shooting style and subsequent skills in handling the carcass are a joy to see. Down the years I have aspired to achieve such expertise but have never succeeded in even approaching them. In mitigation, I should perhaps add that not many of my guests are fit to lick the same plate as these master stalkers, and there are just a few who have been complete nightmares.

On first taking on the deer management at Eve, I offered to host a couple of cull mornings for members of a large stalking group. The arrangement was that I would give a few members of the group a morning's high seat stalking for which they were required to pay a nominal cap of £10 each. The money from the cap was for the Group's funds not for myself. I duly met four or five members (none of whom were previously known to me) and allocated them high seats with a reminder that they were only to shoot from these. I got them all out on the ground before daylight came and when it did, it brought with it a cold, dank, drizzling February morning. Although not my fault in anyway, it was to say the least unpromising and very few deer were seen by the rifles. At the end of the outing, I collected my stalker guests, only one of whom had actually seen deer at all. This chap then said he had planned to get down from his high seat with the intention of stalking the deer he had seen. He also expressed the view that the cap was a rip off, and was reluctant to pay it. When arrangements for another morning visit were being discussed he said he would not be attending because he was stalking elsewhere. I was relieved by that as otherwise I would have had to tell him not to come again. Whilst I was dealing with this, the Eve Estate gamekeeper turned up and another of the guests immediately introduced himself and very obviously started ingratiating himself in the hope or belief that the gamekeeper would be able to arrange for his future stalking on the Estate. I couldn't believe it! I gave those who wanted it another morning. The weather was slightly better and one or two deer were culled, but I was pretty unimpressed with that behaviour and so made my excuses the following year when it was suggested that the scheme might be repeated. There are always one or two "merchants" who spoil it for the rest of the crew.

I knew another man who was apparently keen on deer stalking. Right from the start his attitude worried me. It was, for example, Eve Estate policy for visiting deer stalkers to have at least the entry level Deerstalking Certificate or equivalent qualification. This was not onerous and, in any event a sensible, flexible view was taken if a beginner or occasional stalker was to be taken out under my supervision. This was not the case with this chap. He was an experienced self-taught deerstalker. He simply wouldn't obtain a Certificate.

Another guest stalker who didn't overly impress me was the chap who appeared on a deer moving day, having been introduced by a mutual friend rather than directly invited by myself. He was said to be a very expert rifleman. He probably was that, but I didn't take to the way he appeared to be sizing up the estate's stalking potential and the opportunities he might have on it. I believe he was trying to make a living out of being a "professional" stalker.

Another occasional guest was a very experienced and successful deerstalker and, as were all guests, he was well briefed as to what he could and couldn't shoot. On one visit, he was told that he could shoot all the muntjac he saw. He was allocated a high seat that morning which was situated on the outside of a big woodland block. Eighty yards to the left of this seat was a good, big game strip separated by a strip of short grass from the woodland edge. The deerstalker in this seat could turn half left and comfortably shoot deer on that strip, but needed to be quick as the muntjac coming out of the forestry into the wood did not hang around in the open. The guest was also briefed on these features.

Shortly after the coming of the shooting light, a single shot was heard and then, at intervals others. The sounds of this personal battle continued until the agreed 9.30a.m. finish, by which time there were no less than six muntjac lying on and around the grass strip. Since then I have wondered whether six muntjac in one outing from one high seat is some sort of record. I would add that a week before this man's visit I had culled a couple of muntjac from the same seat and had called a halt so as not to shoot out the stock before the guest came. The six muntjac had to be carried out some distance on foot and the recovery team were sick of the sight of them by the time they had recovered all the carcasses to the road. However, that was nothing to the next amusing recovery problem that this fellow instigated.

There is another farm called Clay Farm quite close to Eve and I undertook (and still undertake) some deer culling on it, trying to catch out deer from the back of the sanctuary to which I have referred earlier. The owner of Clay Farm took a different line over the fallow deer coming on to it. Whereas on the Eve Estate the owner's instructions to me were not to shoot any trophy deer, all and any fallow deer could be culled on Clay Farm. This instruction was all well and good but few if any fallow deer actually resided in the small woods on Clay Farm and the numerous footprints and other signs of them were the result of their nocturnal raids. They were routinely in and out of Clay Farm during the hours of darkness.

In August and September, however, the fallow deer would occasionally emerge from the safety of the sanctuary to gorge on the standing wheat. I erected high seats to deal with these marauders including one seat which was secured to a lone oak tree in the middle of the largest wheat field. Like so many lean to high seats this was not in an absolutely ideal spot, being so far from the woodland edge that the fallow could come out to graze the wheat without ever coming within range of the rifle.

On the August evening in question, the expert guest was sent to this seat with a brief to shoot as many fallow deer as he liked without reference to their size, heads or other qualities. He had to walk up a wheeling through the standing corn to get to the seat and settled in to watch the field in front of him, in the hope that beasts would come out of the wood towards him. In the event he had some good luck as just before darkness fell a small batchelor party of fallow emerged from the more distant woodland on his right hand side and made to cross in front of him through the wheat. This party included a massive buck, which dwarfed several other big beasts. The guest claimed afterwards that he was unable to shoot the big fellow for some reason but that did not prevent him from accounting for two of the big companions, later to hang on the hook, head and legs off, at 150 and 175 lbs respectively. These two animals fell way out in the wheat and had to be recovered with minimum damage through that standing crop. Each one had to come whole and ungralloched along a wheeling, a drag of around four hundred yards a time. Such was their size that two journeys were required to get them over to the deer larder at Eve, which was used for the Clay Farm carcasses. The exhausted expert was finally brought home to bed at sometime after 2a.m. the next morning. I have noticed he has declined all invitations since and understand him to say he is greatly enjoying his roe deer stalking in Wiltshire . Given the extraction problems with a multiple muntjac cull and his right and left of heavy fallow, I can't say I blame him for restricting himself to small deer that can be readily recovered by a lighter drag or in the ubiquitous roe sac.

One chap I liked was a true countryman – and by no means all deerstalkers are that – who had taken up woodland stalking after a lifetime of rough and game shooting. I formed the impression that most of this chap's deer stalking aspirations were focused on visits to the caravan on the coast which he and his stalking partner would visit for a night or two. This was their routine when they stalked the forestry block over which one or both of them had the rights. This, I think, made a very nice little break for them both from their domestic lives. Robert- having started stalking when he was quite old and also in indifferent health - cheerfully acknowledged he was never going to set the stalking world on fire. However, he greatly appreciated an invitation and enjoyed getting out. One cold morning, I inserted him into a low seat in a compartment of conifers behind the yard at Eve. I thought it was a good place for him as the seat was only a short walk away from his parked car. After stalking that morning I returned to the yard to find Robert fast asleep inside his car with a big, old dog fox outside it. When he woke up, Robert told me he had shot the dog fox as it hunted the forest floor and had then decided to pack up and return to his car for a sleep as he was cold. He got another invitation the following summer. For all his light hearted attitude to it, Robert was, one could say, a regular low ground deer stalker compared with one or two men I entertained.

Alastair was an orthopaedic surgeon and a well respected man. His love was hill stalking in Scotland where he stalked stags and hinds in season. Under the tutelage and with the encouragement of the Perthshire hill stalkers he acquired his own deer rifle, although he never used it in England until I took him to Eve Estate one morning. He undoubtedly found our methods foreign to all he had been taught. He was used to stalking deer, whereas we were trying to ambush them. As a well built and then quite elderly man, he found the business of getting up into a high seat quietly a little difficult. He didn't get a shot that morning, which is one I remember because, unusually, I shot two fallow does off my bipod on a winter stubble field.   Alastair enjoyed his morning notwithstanding his lack of success and helped with the larder work. In a charming thank you letter he expressed his appreciation of what he was generous enough to describe as my thoroughly professional set up and I was very pleased by that as he used to go out with some serious stalkers in Scotland. Sadly, it's several years since Alastair has left us, but I hold a happy memory of him that morning dressed in traditional tweeds and enjoying what was for him a novel morning's sport.

Another friend of mine, still very much in his prime, is now the owner of the Bavarian mountain hound bitch which I have mentioned earlier. We could certainly have done with her help on John's first visit.

He came that first time in early November and on his first morning we sat up in our respective high seats without either of us having a shot. I then took John to a high seat overlooking a deer lawn, the grass on which had been topped a month or so previously. I explained my plan to him, which was a simple one. I was to leave him in the seat, walk round the outside of the wood and back to him down wind letting my scent move any deer towards him. I departed on my mission and had not gone far when I heard a shot, which was much too soon to have been fired at any of the deer I was hoping to move. I carried on and having reached the end of the wood walked back towards John's high seat with the wind in my back. When I emerged, John explained that no sooner had I left him than a fallow doe and calf had appeared on the deer lawn from the woodland on the opposite side from which I was intending to move the deer. Not being one to look a gift horse in the face, John had engaged the doe. After the shot she had run back in the direction from which she had appeared together with her calf, without apparently making any other reaction.

I enquired whether he had got her but he was not to be drawn on that. John took me to the spot where he thought she had stood and we examined it thoroughly, but could see no sign that two beasts had ever stood there let alone that one had been shot. Coarse grass of that length is of course a poor surface on which to find paint and pins but I thought that after an engine room shot at seventy yards there should surely be some sign be it blood or hair. I didn't see how John could have missed completely. After a prolonged and microscopic exami-nation of the grass, John and I went into the wood and searched there, where there was still a good deal of under storey and summer vegetation. John still seemed non-committal about his shot and I brought my dog into assist without high hopes of finding her. That was a dog I did not trust and I kept it on a lead whilst he made a rather half hearted search without success. By then the prospects of recovering this doe looked poor. It was sometime after this that John, having widened the search area, found her. She had run seventy or eighty yards and had collapsed in heavy cover. It was a happy guest and host who admired that beast with, I suspect, much mutual relief as to the successful outcome.

Since then John has visited regularly and I have greatly enjoyed stalking with him, as he is a knowledgeable and successful operator with quite as much enthusiasm as I have for the pursuit. He is also a neat and tidy man with all his clothes and kit always spick and span. Aside from the serious help he gives me with my doe culls, we have had and continue to have some amusing times. One of these occurred during a visit he made one May for the roe bucks. Before our first evening outing I explained he must not shoot the German's roe buck. By this I meant the mature roe buck that I had already identified as the beast I wished to save for my friend Carl, who habitually stalked with me for a buck during the rut. As the evening's stalk progressed, I took John round my ground making use of such hedges and ditches as I could to cover our movements. At length we reached a bank from the top of which I knew we could see and, if the opportunity arose, shoot to left or right. I indicated to John to crawl up the bank first and, as soon as he had his head over the top, became aware of him tensing and pulling himself up on to his elbows and into a shooting position. No time was wasted; the shot off the bipod was quickly taken and John told me the buck was down on the drilled corn. He didn't tell me which buck, but as soon as I saw the head I knew he had shot the German's buck.

Like the good stalker he is John had seized an opportunistic chance to cull a buck that would otherwise have spooked and made off, and I would have done the same had I had the rifle. However, I wasn't going to tell him that and grumbled a bit on the way home about how I was going to find another head fit for my important and discerning German friend now that John had shot his trophy. My playful mood persisted the next morning when, in the first grey light of the day, I took John by a discreet route to an observation point on an artificial mound overlooking one of my woods. It was still too dark to identify the constituents of this mound but I encouraged John to crawl up to the top of this and to settle down on it's soft, squidgy summit, whilst unfolding and lying on an old piece of groundsheet myself. I had two indifferent bucks in that locality and thought it likely we should spy at least one of them when the light came. Just as I expected, we caught an early glimpse in the half light of a roe buck. At that point he was going away from us but I had every confidence he would return to the wood corner which we commanded. In due course he did and I enjoyed watching John dig his elbows into the soft top of the mound as he tried to find the best available firing point. The buck made the task easy for him in the end, stopping now and then to graze and browse as it approached. Eventually, having chosen his killing zone, John squeezed the trigger and finished the business. As he stood up my broad grin said it all. John's immaculate stalking gear was liberally coated in horse muck. That, I thought, will teach you not to shoot the German's buck!

Amongst the occasional guests that I want to do well by are those who buy deer stalking outings in charity auctions. I once donated a lot in an auction of promises being held to assist some unfortunate young soldier and my lot was, I believe, promoted with outrageous puff as an early winter morning's low ground stalking followed by an al fresco breakfast. Whatever was represented, I was informed that a young professional man from London had paid a fortune for this lot and it was now down to me to ensure he wasn't disappointed. The first obstacle to achieving this became obvious when I got in touch with Justin who told me that he thought he would put off coming until February as he was rather busy in the office. I explained that it would be even more difficult to show him some sport in February than it would be in early November, and eventually persuaded him to come on the following Friday. That gave me time to tip bags of windfall apples in front of two high seats so that I could take him to whichever one was right for wind, with the hope, if not the expectation, that a deer or two would come to feed on them whilst we were sitting there.

Before dawn on that Friday the weather was unseasonably dry and mild, and Justin met me at the r/v on time. As he was to use my rifle there was no need for a zeroing session. Justin claimed to have shot for his school rifle team so I had to hope that my accurate rifle and his marksmanship would come together and give the right result. It wasn't ideal but the best I could do and, in any event, I would be at his shoulder to veto any risky shots. I had him dry fire the rifle when we reached the stalking ground so that he could test the pull of the trigger. Then I took him to the high seat in the wood and settled him down to await the light.

As we sat there with the passing morning minutes squeezing the darkness out of the sky I was observing the scene regularly through my binoculars. It wasn't very long before I became aware of a deer at the apples. As it got lighter still I could see he was a fallow deer and that he was scoffing apples as fast as he could, even bending his head back over his shoulders to guzzle the apples more quickly than he otherwise could. I silently indicated the animal to my client and his eyes nearly popped out of his head when he saw the size of him. By sheer good luck the pricket- that is what he was- came out into the open at that point and presented a simple shot which was well taken. The two of us then dragged the beast out to the wood's edge and I demonstrated a gralloch by the pond there. I felt a huge sense of relief at performing my part of the bargain so easily and early. I then told Justin we would walk and stalk in another wood, and in the next hour was able to show him roe and muntjac deer, although his inexperienced hasty movements denied him a shot at the former and the latter stood skylined on a raised stoway on the woodland edge. Before packing up I then walked Justin round Fifty Wood where, in the space of a few minutes, we luckily got on terms with a parcel of fallow does, one of which he shot.

It was one extremely chuffed young man that I took to the trucker's snack van beside the A11 for bacon rolls and coffee in the sunshine. He was quite delighted with his morning's sport and had really enjoyed his first experience of woodland stalking. Before we went our separate ways I gave him some advice. "Never bid for a morning's winter woodland stalking again. You have had the luck of the devil today. Nine times out of ten your morning would have comprised two hours sitting in a dank fog, and then breakfast here whilst being sluiced down with spray water off the trucks on the carriageway!"

Whilst still on the subject of guest stalkers, I have entertained a good many of these who are what I would describe as solid, occasional stalkers. They certainly don't want to be committed to achieving a regular cull but they like an outing now and then perhaps for prickets in the early autumn and again for does in November, before conditions become too severe. One of these shot a right and left of prickets one night. Another accounted for a fallow doe and was distressed that it ran fifty yards from the place where it was shot. I had to explain this was quite normal in the case of a deer shot in the heart or lungs and that his had not been a bad shot at all.

I have also taken out a few European stalkers. To a man, they have been amazed by the amount and variety of our wildlife and game and after talking to them about the poor position of game shooting in Germany , just for example, I must say we are incredibly lucky here that thus far small game shooting has not been wrecked in the same way. I took one German friend with me to witness the transfer of pheasant poults into a release pen and he watched open mouthed when a thousand poults walked out of their crates and started exploring their new home.

Continental stalkers appear to unduly favour roe buck stalking in the rut. I consider the prime month for them to be May. Many are preoccupied with shooting deer with antlers for their antlers and are not prepared to make an adequate management cull of female deer. These points on one side, I do not find much to distinguish Continental from English stalkers. Some are excellent shots; others have lesser ability. Some are competent stalkers; other mere bunglers. As with our own fraternity they come in all shapes and sizes and have varying levels of enthusiasm and fitness for deerstalking. In saying this I acknowledge that none of my guests pay for their stalking so, for this if no other reason, are probably on their best behaviour.

I have mentioned above the shooting of Carl's buck by my good friend John. Without taking it too seriously, one of the constructive aspects of Carl's visits are that they cause me to prepare for them by checking on my bucks during the spring in order to identify and select a suitable one for him. I can then watch out for that animal and ascertain his habits and movements and plan a stalk on him.

One summer I had a really ripe old timer reserved for Carl and well recall the thrilling rut time stalk we had down a sunken lane through seven or eight other deer. I don't know to this day how we negotiated our way down that track without spooking the lot or how we crawled in unseen through the grass for the last fifty yards and reached a firing point with the old buck still lying down. That really was a memorable stalk and Carl took a trophy head home to Cologne as a permanent memento that morning's stalking.

One summer, I identified a splendid buck for my friend. This was a buck of remarkably regular habits which most early mornings made a perambulation of his territory, which included a visit to the Bourn trout pond. The grass and herbs grew lush around this and he would routinely spend a few minutes grazing on these. As a certain amount of mowing was done here throughout the summer to facilitate the fishing, it would have been possible for my friend to see and shoot this buck from a temporary high seat. This could have been secured to one of the trees around the lake - a pretty spot from which to watch and wait for a roe buck. I had a plan but, when my friend could not come, had no wish to shoot that buck myself.

The last category of guests I mainly recall with pleasure are complete beginners. Young men and women, perhaps with a back-ground in game shooting, sometimes express an interest in my curious pursuit, perhaps thinking that as I spend so much time at it there must be something in it that makes it worthwhile. If they press, I will take these individuals out so they can see how I go on. One man,whom I met at 3.30am on a Saturday morning in June, enjoyed the morning in which we saw three species of deer and, under my supervision, shot a decent muntjac buck. He enjoyed himself, but rising at that hour when a man has toddlers at home and a full time full on, high pressure job does not make for a happy combination. The serious, regular deerstalker simply really cannot handle such commitments.

I can well remember the time when I had my own solicitor's practice. After an early morning start and stalk I would often go into my office, change into a suit and have some coffee there. The mornings were not too bad but afternoons were a gritty eyed misery as the 3a.m. start began to catch up with me. I was probably foolish to pursue my stalking so relentlessly at that stage of my professional career but must say now that the fun and sport I had more than justified it. As to the occasional roe buck or muntjac carcass that I hung in the cool of my office strong room (to the horror of my more squeamish staff) I can only say how sorry I am now for any distress I caused. My enthusiasm got the better of me at the time.

Chapter Fifteen

Foxes, Other Animals and Invertebrates

I N MY YOUTH, father instructed me that foxes were for hunting not for shooting. He applauded the land owner who on employing a new keeper allegedly inscribed in red ink and capital letters the front of his contract with the legend: "FOXES COME FIRST". As this story dated from the English Partridge era I have great doubts as to it's authenticity. Unless foxes were rare in that locality at that time I do not consider any grey partridge keeper worth his salt would have tolerated foxes on his manor.

Nonetheless, this was the ethos in which I grew up. I cannot recall any of the owners of the game shoots which I attended allowing foxes to be shot by the guns on a formal shoot day, even though the shoot keeper may very likely have been discreetly dealing with them at other times. Father and I followed the hounds by car and I enjoyed being a car follower for the amusing company it provided and the very occasional view of a hunted fox. For one season, just after I had passed my driving test, I acted as an occasional amateur terrier man and remember the fox terrier, that belonged to the young whipper-in, bolting one particularly large dog fox from a drain. Over the years, I have bolted and dug other foxes with the assistance of a number of borrowed terriers and have enjoyed occasional terrier work. This is a rural pursuit in it's own right, in addition to being a valuable service to farmers, game keepers and poultrymen. I have also snared and lamped foxes.

However, it was not until I took up low ground stalking that I started shooting foxes regularly with the rifle. It was only when I changed my lifestyle to suit the needs of low ground stalking, when I had to be out in the fields and woods at around first and last light, that I began to appreciate the large number of foxes that there are in them. As I acquired stalking rights over various farms, I always made a point of ascertaining the landowner's attitude towards foxes. From my point of view I was not seriously troubled by foxes, provided they were not in the vicinity of my game and rough shoots. I did not particularly want to shoot foxes early in a deerstalking outing and, through the noise of the shot, spoil my best or even only chance of a deer.

Whatever my scruples and my grudging admiration for the fox as a smart animal, most of my landowners and their keepers wanted me to shoot on sight any foxes that I encountered. I was usually instructed that there was a zero tolerance policy towards foxes, although not always in those words. On the basis that the deer manager is the steward of the landowner, I then resolved that when instructed by the landowner to shoot foxes on his land that is what I must do and do effectively. This led to my developing the interesting and exciting pursuit of daylight fox shooting. During the period I have been undertaking low ground deer management, the majority of foxes culled in these parts have been lamped, called and shot with centre fire rifles at night. With the law relating to deer limiting the legal hours of deer shooting to those from one hour before sunrise to one hour after sunset, I am rarely on the ground during the hours of darkness and so do not carry or use the lamp. Any fox I see will be out and about during the hours of daylight, although of course it is usually at first or last light. I have had many interesting encounters with foxes during my outings and have seen literally hundreds of them in many different locations and circumstances.

By far the most pleasing shot at a fox I have had occurred last year on a small shoot near my home. The farm it is on comprises fields that slope quite steeply down to a stream with high, overgrown banks. These are a haven for wildlife, game and foxes. The fields themselves are grass pastures and are grazed in rotation for cattle during the summer. On the morning of the incident giving rise to this anecdote

I was prowling along the side of the stream observing the low ground in front of me and the grass pasture on the hill to my left. I was taking it very slowly in true stalking mode. I was walking fifty paces and stopping to spy and then repeating this so slowly, it was, as some say, like watching paint dry. In one of the pauses, I became aware of an animal dropping down off the hill top and coming towards me at what I would describe as a brisk walking pace. I say "became aware" because in the sepia half light of the early morning that's how it was rather than me clearly seeing it.

With the assistance of my binoculars, I identified the animal as a fox and could also see that it was carrying a large object. With the fox still coming down towards me, I opened my shooting sticks and set them up and in the same slow movement rested the forend of my rifle in the fork of them. The fox came on and then obligingly stopped and sat on his haunches, perhaps resting on account of his heavy load. I squeezed the trigger gently and he collapsed. With the echo of the single shot resonating around the hill, I walked up to him and found him to be a moderately sized dog fox which was carrying a half grown and partly eaten muntjac carcass.

I left both fox and muntjac remains by the gate to the pheasant pen with a note to the effect that there was most likely an earth with cubs in the bank of the stream. The last place the keeper of this small shoot needed a fox was in this low ground around his young birds. This is the only occasion on which I have encountered a fox with a muntjac and I wish very much that I could confirm that this fox had killed the muntjac rather than, say, picking up a road traffic accident casualty. I have little doubt that the fox did kill the muntjac it was carrying, as it was a fresh carcass with no other sign of injury. However, I could not be absolutely certain this was the case. I know for sure that there are occasions when foxes alarm muntjac and, if I hear muntjac barking, I automatically now anticipate the appearance of a fox. It follows that foxes must give muntjac cause for alarm and the most likely way they do this is by predating on kids and partly grown muntjac such as the one I examined.

Another interesting fox was the one I called the Twenty Wood Vixen. I first encountered her on the deer lawn in Twenty Wood on which, from her actions that morning , I would say she was hunting

128

for mice or voles.. She was extremely distinctive being a small, neat vixen, having a large white bib like a corgi dog. Foxes are always amusing to watch when they are mousing, as they are a study in concentration, with all their senses focused on the hunt. As there was no game shoot around Twenty Wood at that time I was not under any pressure to shoot this animal then and decided to observe it and try to find out more about it. That morning, she hunted unsuccessfully and eventually, quite late in the morning, left the deer lawn as if she intended to head for the forestry block two fields away. In the following weeks I saw the Twenty Wood Vixen on three more occasions in Twenty Wood, and she was hunting or travelling on each of these. I formed the impression she was not resident in Twenty Wood but came into it for food. Then, one morning, I was sitting up on the edge of the forestry block in a position that enabled me to monitor the watercourse that flowed from the forest across two fields and into the bottom compartment in Twenty Wood. I recall I had had a blank morning and that the roe buck I was hoping to catch coming back to the forestry had not returned. The morning was getting well advanced for deer stalking purposes anyway, and I was thinking about getting down, when I caught sight of an animal trotting along the brew of the ditch towards my high seat. With the binoculars I was soon able to identify her as the Twenty Wood vixen. She was carrying a half grown rabbit in her mouth which confirmed she was, as I thought, a resident of the forestry who habitually hunted away from home.

On evening outings, I have sometimes seen two or even three foxes leave this forestry and surge through the drilled wheat towards Twenty Wood at the start of an evening's hunting. Watching them through binoculars, the deerstalker can't help but be impressed by the predatory power of the fox and the aura of lethality they carry when compared with the scatter brained hare of the skittish rabbit.

I carry a number of calls that (sometimes) attract foxes. I have a tiny, high pitched mouse squeak call. My widgeon caller is one that is widely used and although mine is commercially manufactured some fox shooting enthusiasts make up their own more economically from beer bottle tops. I also have a black plastic reed call that generates a loud squeal calculated to bring the wariest fox into rifle range. If I see a fox which is within hearing distance, I will often select one of these. I try to squeak the fox in so that I can shoot it. On one of the shoots on which I undertake the deer control, I was sitting outside the pheasant release pen one summer evening when I became aware of a fox on the track on the outside of the wood. I lay down on the track with my rifle on a clip-on bipod and squeaked this vixen (for that is what she was) with the mouse call. She turned towards the sound, and came fast, so fast that I had to shout to stop her. Then I shot her.

The old keeper was curmudgeonly about it, because she had cubs, but I took the view that with fifteen hundred pheasants to pen, he could not afford to house a vixen and hungry cubs.

In the proximity of the Bourn stream, fox calling can prove unproductive because the fox cannot hear the calls over the sound of the running water. One windy morning, a dog fox appeared in the corner of the wood overlooking the bourn, where I was concealed in ambush. He stood on a small mound surveying the scene and gave every appearance of being hungry. I started with the mouse call, but elicited no reaction at all. Then, I tried the widgeon call, which made a much louder squeal. The fox heard that and came out to investigate. When he reached a fallen tree butt I used that as a back stop for the shot that killed him.

One evening, on another farm, I was sitting up in a high seat one summer evening without any specific quarry in mind. This was a field seat in the angle formed by the juncture of two hedges. There were grass strips running both ways and a crop of wheat about a foot high with distinct tractor wheelings in it. There was a badger sett some seventy yards in front of the seat, which was often but not always used by the local badgers. As I sat quietly there enjoying a pleasantly warm summer evening I became aware of fox cubs on the grass strip. Five cubs in all, the size of cats, were playing, scuffling and enjoying life on the lawn outside the accommodation their mother had borrowed from the badgers. I could have engaged all these cubs at some point during the proceedings but that was not my way. If I shot one or two cubs the vixen would move the rest of them for sure. The next night I came back and sat up in good time with my rifle. The evening ebbed slowly away and, as the light began to go, the cubs tumbled out to play and, I hoped, to welcome their mother. It was late when she came, fast and silently, and I let her settle and see to the cubs before giving her a couple of squeaks. She jumped clear of the cubs and came fast down the wheeling in response. It may sound hard nosed but I shot her, and then waited several more nights for the dog fox. Fox cubs are hardy young creatures and the extended fox family in the form of the dog fox father and the aunties of the cubs take over the feeding of the cubs. Having failed to account for that dog fox, I snared both him and the surviving cubs in the autumn in very close proximity to my pheasant pen.

My friends who lamp foxes regularly tell me that they encounter many lamp shy and call shy foxes. Plainly these must have been "educated" by lampers misusing the lamp, by overcalling in an area and by carelessness such as a lack of attention to wind direction. All I can say is that in my experience foxes respond well to the call in day time providing they can hear it and that the wind is not blowing the stalker's scent to them. I would go so far as to say that sitting up in high seats for the purpose of calling and shooting foxes is productive at first and last light and is perhaps a method that more game keepers and fox controllers should consider using.

Another species of animal that I have seen from time to time is the badger. The most striking feature of any badger is not it's distinctive black and white coat but the speed at which it moves. Brain washed by "Wind in the Willows" I believe the public tend to imagine "Mr. Badger" as a carpet slippers and pipe sort of animal. Far from it! All the badgers I have seen have been active and fast on their feet. I had one cross a clearing in front of me when I was sitting up in a sweet chestnut tree near the Suffolk coast. He came across the open ground at the run and only slowed down when he reached cover on my side of it. Even then he was moving about in an active manner and soon disappeared from view under the top canopy.

There are badger setts on the Eve Estate and one of these happens to be in a hillside belt at the bottom of which I have a high seat, which is strategically placed to catch out the passing trade of roe and muntjac deer. The seat is there to pick them up as they travel via a linking belt between the hillside belt and the main wood in the valley. One early morning, I watched a sow badger returning to the sett at the gallop across drilled corn and the young maize plants of a game strip. Again, it was the sense of purpose and speed of this animal that impressed and surprised me. She was in no way slow!

Two badgers appeared one misty morning on the woodland edge in front of this high seat. The smaller of the two was barging and harassing the other one as they scuttled along the wood margin. It seemed that the one inflicting the harassment was a young male and probably the son of the sow. That incident gave me an amusing insight into domestic violence in the badger family.

Another sett on the Eve Estate is strangely situated at the junction of two hedges on the heavy land. Badgers have been established there for several years and now and then, in the course of my stalking activities, I have seen them above ground. I always approach the sett cautiously in case there is one about. On one particular occasion, I did not see a badger, but saw a lot of steam or condensation coming off freshly turned earth. Whether this came off a badger or the soil I could not say but the sight of the steam emanating from the mouth of this hole on a frosty morning was bizarre. On another day, when this same hole came into view as I walked round the corner of the hedge, a badger's ample backside was sticking out of one of the holes. I watched with interest for a few minutes until the backside's owner and the backside disappeared underground.

The gamekeeper on the Eve Estate is adamant that the estate is visited by a big cat or cats in the form of a puma. Over the years he has shown me a number of deer carcasses, most of them reduced to little more than desiccated skin and bones. The skin on these has been rolled up rather like a roll of paper or foil, which he informs me is characteristic of a puma's consumption of a carcass. The carcasses have been found in unusual places, such as in the middle of big, open fields, which suggests the deer whose carcass it is may have been chased, hunted down, killed and eaten in the open, which, again, is I understand typical of a puma's modus operandi. He has also noted that when he is finding fresh carcasses, the deer on the Eve Estate are either jittery and nervous or even conspicuous by their absence.

At least one of the tractor drivers on the estate says he has seen the puma on two separate occasions. The first time he saw it, the puma was in a grass strip. On the second occasion he says he saw it on a wood corner watching a woman taking a walk. It was, he said, very attentive of the walker. By coincidence, another landowning friend of mine (living thirty miles away from Eve), who is a countryman, farmer and pheasant shoot operator of great experience, told me that one summer a puma was seen at least twice by their keeper whilst he was out lamping. For a few days, around this time, his wife experienced their dogs growling in a suppressed and scared manner when she took them past a certain wood in the course of her daily walk.

These accounts come from reliable witnesses who have nothing to gain from telling shaggy cat stories.

If there really is a puma I wish I could see it. I understand the puma is by nature nocturnal and also discreet. If this be so, with my being about the woods and fields in the quiet hours around dawn and dusk, I should see one if anyone does. I can say this with confidence, based on all the hours I have sat up in high seats and watched deer and other wildlife carrying on their affairs undisturbed and unaware of my presence. I am habitually observing them from well concealed positions. The deer and other mammals do not as a rule see or sense me so neither should a puma. As the ambushes I stage are often overlooking hedges and ditches between woods on the Eve Estate and these are conduits for the local deer moving between them then a puma should use these too. If there is just one puma, with a huge range, perhaps the chances of even a person out on the ground as often as I am has only an outside chance of seeing it.

I did see an animal one night which looked like a puma. The circumstances were that I was driving home in the dark after a winter evening's stalking at Eve. After travelling about five miles and passing through a village I was in a mile long stretch in stud country. In the headlights of my truck I saw a big catlike animal jump the newly planted roadside hedge. It took the post and rail stud fence in another near vertical jump in which it's feet and legs were deliberately used to give the animal a spring board off the top rail. That was all I saw as by then I had passed the spot where it was, with my lights by then being directed further along the road. So fleeting was my view that I cannot give any credence to what I think I saw or even say for sure that I saw a puma at all. If it was a domestic cat, which is most likely, it was certainly a giant of the species.

I can accept that captive puma may have been released: individuals always have and always will release animals. I recognise that puma may have escaped from captivity: animals always have escaped and always will. I find much of the evidence I hear on the subject persuasive and acknowledge that those who have deposed to it are reliable witnesses. In spite of all this I am in the final analysis unprepared to say there is a big cat at large in Suffolk or any other part of the U.K until I see one with my own eyes. I can only hope against hope that in the clear early light of some summer morning I shall see a sandy coated puma slinking along a grass strip towards my high seat or stalking an unsuspecting deer on the woodland edge.

In assessing the very small chances of seeing a big cat, I can make a comparison with the rare sightings of red deer I have had during my low ground stalking career. I have not seen any of this species on or even near my stalking grounds for at least five years. I once saw three red deer at Three Valleys. They passed through one August and then disappeared as if they had never been there. On the Eve Estate, during my first season, I heard an amusing story from the retired gamekeeper who had been on the Estate for his whole working life. In that autumn, having found fraying in one of the light land belts I enquired of him whether there could be any red deer on the Estate. His prompt reply was that that was the visiting card of the Quendon Stag. He explained that as a young, naive underkeeper, many years earlier, he had one September day encountered a massive animal in that very belt and, being frightened by it, had reported the sighting to the then head keeper. That, he had been told was the stag that made it's way to Quendon before every rut and returned whence it had come at the end of it. Quendon was and is some miles distant from Eve. If the red deer that did the fraying I saw was the current Quendon Stag then he would have been a successor of the original one by many generations.

A few years later, when the corn crops were ready for harvest, I went to the adjacent belt to check zero on my rifle. There, in the standing wheat, was a very decent stag . Perhaps that was the

Quendon stag! I once saw a superb stag in standing wheat on one of Eve's heavy land farms but those are the only four red deer I have ever seen there. This is strange because within fifteen miles there are significant populations of red deer which, subject to crossing main roads and railway lines, could readily travel to any of the areas in which I operate.

The effect of their absence, as far as my own stalking goes, is that I do not as a rule stalk low ground red deer and have never shot a red deer in Suffolk. I have stalked and shot red deer in the rut in Devon and Cornwall and had some exciting times down there.

My guide and stalker was the well known Pat Carey alias "the Warrener". Pat was and, indeed, still is a most enterprising and interesting countryman who has made his living as a fox controller, and through providing country pursuits such as rough shooting and deer stalking and other related activities such as the making and selling of instruction videos on fox control.

Pat had and has deer stalking rights over large tracts of land with the species present there being red and roe deer. As I have said, I went, as a very inexperienced stalker, to stalk a red deer stag. I found Pat's approach very interesting as his deer stalking technique was highly pro-active. He lived in a small village and enjoyed the stalking rights over a substantial plantation a few hundred yards from his house. There were red stags in this woodland and, before my arrival, Pat had, he said, smeared some form of attractant around the main wallow. I believe this attractant was intended for use against whitetail deer in the U.S.A. Whatever it's origin and intended target, it certainly had a dramatic effect on Pat's red deer. On entering the woodland, we were nearly knocked down by one stag and, in the course of an hour or so encountered two others. Stags were rushing around the wood, appearing and disappearing as, presumably, the big beasts tried to chase away their lesser challengers.

On a subsequent visit, Pat took me into Cornwall, where he had the sporting rights over a stock farm, the lower, steeper slopes of which were well wooded with hardwoods and a plantation of larch. The river running through the valley was fast flowing and attractive as it ran through lush, grass pastures with the woodland rising on the far side of it. Visiting this farm on the top of the day, we walked round until Pat found a rutting stand on the very edge of the wood. This he baited with his patent lure. We returned the following morning, well before it was light, and tucked into the cover on the river bank, our backs to the river and our faces towards the rutting stand eighty or a hundred yards away across the grass. No deer of any species or description appeared which, I could tell, surprised Pat. He felt strongly that his ploy should have worked. Although that gambit was unsuccessful, I took something away from it far better than a stag. This was Pat's whispered comment to me as the pre dawn dark eased. In his broad Devonian accent he said: "The light, the light, she's coming fast now!" Over many years, I have recited that phrase to myself time and again in many different locations and have always found it to evoke the magic of a morning outing after deer, just as it did that morning in the meadow beside that fast flowing river.

Pat's next move was to identify any deer tracks between the wood and the higher fields, above the larch plantation. Walking the outside edge of this we eventually found several strong, fresh tracks. Red deer were clearly using these regularly to gain access to and from the fields and the plantation. The field next to the larches sloped downhill from right to left and had, at the top of it, and just outside the plantation, a stack of big black bagged silage bales. These might have been purpose built as a near perfect observation and firing point. It was arranged that I would sit up on these bags that evening. I was back there in good time and settled down to watch the field from a position in which I could sit or kneel on the bottom tier of bales and be hidden by the second tier. I planned to take a kneeling shot if the chance arose using the top of the second tier of bale bags as a rest.

I had not been waiting long when a parcel of hinds stepped out of the larches and walked just in front of me. They were followed into the field by a stocky, thickset stag. He, too, was just a few yards in front of me. Hardly daring to raise myself at all I pointed the rifle at the stag and fired. The stag and hinds ran back into the larch plantation. My reaction to my self evident miss was one of disbelief until I saw that I had shot a channel through the top of the silage bale in front of me. I had made that classic beginner's error of omitting to check that I had a clear line of fire as well as a clear line of sight. If there was any justice in the world that would or should have been the end of my sport for the evening, but it was not at all.

A few minutes later another parcel of hinds streamed out on to the field in front of me followed by a much larger stag with what even I could tell was an excellent head. By now I had the rifle raised and resting on my binoculars, and aimed it nearly half way up his chest and just behind his front leg. I squeezed the trigger and he turned into the shot before making off at speed into the larches. When Pat rejoined me , I explained what had happened and we went forward together and looked into the larches below us. It was the steam from the fallen stag which showed us where he lay. We ran down to him and looked at the huge animal. Pat then looked up towards the field high above us and, thinking about extraction, groaned: "Oh David! Whatever have you shot?"

I dare say every sanctimonious deer manager in the country will say I should never have engaged that stag. They would point out piously that he was the father of that herd and that his role was or should have been to disseminate his seed. I do not dispute any of this; in fact, I agree with it all.

I had never shot a Royal stag before and have not and never will shoot another one now. Indeed in all the male deer I shoot I take more satisfaction in accounting for a cull beast than in killing any number of trophies. This said, I have no regrets about the shooting of that stag. At the time, in the heat of a hunter's excitement, I heard the hunter's horn call loud and clear. I would have him! And I did.

The great head still has pride of place in my home and every day rekindles the excitement and thrill of the woodland stalking in that place, and the sweet success that was all the sweeter after the miss caused by my own inept tyro's mistake.

Turning to sika deer, I have only stalked these on high ground and so have no experience of them in a low ground context. The large population of sika in Dorset's Poole Basin allegedly create environmental problems just as fallow in East Anglia are said to do. However, both species also provide opportunities for good, interesting and at times exciting sport.

Another "must do before I die!" is to stalk a Chinese Water Deer.

Having observed these attractive looking little deer on a shoot days and also during a deer watch in Bedfordshire I would like to hunt at least one and to acquire a representative head for my modest trophy collection.

Much is made of the scarcity of hares, but on the farmland over which I stalk in East Anglia there are plenty of hares. It's not unusual for me to observe up to a dozen from one high seat vantage point in the course of a morning or evening. Quite a lot of hares live in woodland and, by sitting quietly over the woodland edge, the deerstalker gains an insight of the hare traffic between the woods and fields. Hares give the deerstalker great pleasure as their antics are very entertaining. I once watched a hare taking a sand bath one sunny morning and was greatly amused by the way in which it rolled and wriggled in the sun dried sand of a field bank.

Foxes appear to acknowledge that hares are too fast for them and several times I have watched a fox ignoring a number of hares as he crosses a field during his evening's hunting. In the snow this winter, I watched a hare putting on his parts close to a ditch from which eventually emerged a fox, obviously disappointed by the failure of his attempted stalk. The hare moved away from the ditch and the hungry fox sat for some minutes on the brew of it visibly disappointed by his failed effort.

The rabbit is a reliable indicator as to when a fox is about. In numbers they graze off the crops close to hedges and woodland margins and the areas that they keep short are useful places for the deerstalker to watch in high summer. Here he may see and shoot a muntjac or roe buck that just a few yards away would be invisible.

Whilst stalking in the spring and summer, various unpleasant invertebrates may be encountered. I find ticks to be at their worst in April and follow up every outing with a careful self inspection. At worst, I have removed up to a dozen ticks from my person. Close inspection is necessary as they can get anywhere and, not infrequently, are extremely small. Ankle boots, gaiters and a buttoned down shirt and of course a proprietary repellent all serve to deter ticks, but if the deerstalker sits in or crawls through long grass then he increases his chances of picking up ticks.

If he keeps his dogs in the house then they are likely to pick up ticks which may transfer their attentions to humans. I keep my dogs "frontlined" during the spring and summer and also discourage them from going into long grass and cover as far as I practically can.

The effects of Lyme Disease are unpleasant and deerstalkers should be aware of and watch out for the symptoms. One young man I know who contracted it was treated unavailingly for meningitis and only survived after the true cause of his critical condition was recognised by a passing consultant. Several years later he was still suffering from the after effects of the disease. Although Lyme or Weill's Disease can both be very nasty, and indeed fatal, I long ago decided that the they were not going to deter me from deerstalking. In the U.K. attacks on the deerstalker by mosquitoes, midges, horse flies and cleggs can be highly unpleasant, particularly those of midges in summer Scotland but not dangerous. In low ground England, most insects can be kept at bay by the use of suitable clothing, veils and a good repellent. In this respect, the English deerstalker is extremely fortunate to operate in such benign conditions. There really are very few mammals or invertebrates that are likely to harm him and the contrast with hunting in other countries, such as Africa, are stark. This observation is founded on personal experience as, during a week's hunting in Namibia in March 2007, I encountered four snakes, the most proximate of which was a mamba that, although uninvited, joined me in my ground blind and became a touch agitated in the only exit. By way of comparison with such venomous creatures, the occasional wasps nest or rare adder are almost benign.

Chapter Sixteen

Hitting and Missing

I N THE COURSE of last season's game shooting, I can recall a drive in which I shot well by my standards. I shot five partridges and six pheasants without a miss. These were good birds and the other guns who saw me kill them congratulated me on the high standard of my shooting. In retrospect I am afraid that my pride over my brief, purple patch with the shot gun has led to me airbrushing out of my memories my very ordinary if not downright awful shooting throughout the rest of the day and, indeed, most days of the season. I am ashamed to say that I have nearly convinced myself that I shot rather well all season and quite brilliantly during that happy drive.

These thoughts on shooting with the shot gun take me to other points which contrast with the position of the low ground stalker. First, the deerstalker seeks to attain a position and situation in which he can take the easiest shot. If he can engage a deer at fifty yards in good light he is not going to pass on the shot because he may get the opportunity to shoot it at two hundred yards' range in bad light. He seeks and takes the easier shot to be certain of ensuring a clean kill. There is really no equivalent of the "high bird good, low bird bad" mentality of the game shot.

Second, the deerstalker is unhappy if not downright distressed if he wounds a deer. Whilst not wishing to cause any bird suffering, there is no doubt the pricking of game birds is an occasional consequence of shooting at them. Some say that a good team of guns will prick more birds than a bad team because all their shots will be fairly accurate and as far as the target birds are concerned will be there or thereabouts.

My third thought is that we all- stalkers and shooters alike- are prone to puffing up the good shots we make and suppressing the uncomfortable, embarrassing memories of our not-so-good and bad ones.

The words – "position" and "situation"- were in my mind the winter evening I was sitting out late for fallow in the middle of Maytree Farm. The weather was sharp, with hard frosts holding all day, causing the fallow deer on the adjacent estate to visit Maytree Farm by night and creep into the farmyard itself to eat the sugar beet on the heap awaiting transportation to the factory. The farmer was upset by this and had asked me if I could deter them. I walked round in daylight and found the main deer path down the boundary bank opposite the middle ditch. Any fallow deer using this would leave the big wood, walk up the edge of the Estate field under cover of one hedge and come down the bank prior to crossing the open ground and into the farm yard by way of the rectangular spinney. It was, I thought, a typical fallow route- devious, discreet and unknown to anyone except an "on the spot" fallow deerstalker such as myself. I considered waiting in the farmyard itself but thought it would be too dark to shoot by the time the fallow arrived, if they came at all. I therefore decided to wait in the middle ditch looking on to the deer path that was opposite me on the bank of the boundary hedge.

That evening, I slipped into position as the last of the many dog walkers were heading home along the bridleway behind me. Soon after they had gone, the wild life and game on the place began to show. I caught sight of one or two pheasants hurrying back to the big wood- old cock birds by the look of them that had obviously been out gleaning a late afternoon feed. The local hares became more active and I picked up the pale coloured shapes of rabbits on the woodland edge. I watched all this in the fading light, with my loaded rifle on it's bipod already placed where it could be readily shouldered and brought to bear in a firing position with the minimum of movement. If they came, I knew these fallow deer would come late. The only questions were whether they would come at all and, if they did, whether I would be able to see them. I was confident in my position,

141

but unsure whether the situation would allow me a shot. I really needed and wanted a kill that night: the sight of a fallow deer carcass in the back of the truck would cheer my farmer up no end.

As I waited in this ambush place the day was imperceptibly sliding into night. Lights were coming on in the local houses and headlights of cars showing up on the nearby roads. First, the wood and then the bank and hedge in front of me lost definition with the bushes and trees becoming blurred. My tactical thoughts on position and situation surrendered themselves to more indulgent musings on the day just done and days to come.

And then the fallow were on the bank! I could not see deer, but shapes and movement. A shape on top of the bank disappeared from view. My check through the binoculars picked it up on my field, now with the bank behind it, safe to engage if I could see to shoot. I switched from binoculars – heavy light gathering binoculars- to the scope of my rifle. I couldn't see anything and then I screwed down the magnification and got a picture, a broadside shadow of a beast and a dark chest shape. I had scruples; it really was too late, but my farmer wanted a kill. I fired.

There was an explosion of sound and a flash of light and I was blinded for a moment, and recovered my sight to see shapes of beasts fleeing. There was no need to wait. I walked across to the bottom of the bank and there was no beast there. I climbed up the bank and saw a lump on the ground half way back to the wood where there had been no lump before. I went forward and the lump jumped up and ran into the wood before I could fire again. I walked to the wood edge; couldn't see anything. I waited listening; couldn't hear anything. I had to give up on it and went home distraught. I was back at first light with my dog, and permission from the wood's gamekeeper, to make a search. I didn't need the dog. There,under the fir trees, was the cold carcass of a beast, which it transpired had taken a liver shot.

My position had been perfect but my situation had been terrible. Under pressure from the landowner, I had painted myself into a corner and essayed a shot at a near invisible beast. No fine definition to aim at there; just a blur in the dark, a shape in the darkness.

In another place, I enjoyed the evening autumn sunshine full in my face whilst sitting in one of my most productive seats. It was September pricket time and the stubble in front of me was pale and warm and the hedges abundant with food. I had every confidence the fallow would come, and so they did when the sun went down. There was the usual parcel with an old lead doe and, at the rear, a sorrel and a pricket. I was sure I would shoot the pricket to join the long list of beasts shot from this seat. Casually, much too casually, I aimed and fired and the pricket jumped and ran with the rest, ran away to the other side of the estate, then stopped and went on more slowly behind the rest now, carrying a foreleg. By great good fortune, I had another rifle there. I called him on the radio: "Get up to the wood corner fast; run!run!run!", I instructed.

I could see him, a far away figure, getting there fast, heard the sound of a shot and then got the good news. He had collected the runner. "Mea culpa!"was the order of the evening for me; self reproach and shame at fluffing so simple a shot. Pride cometh before a fall…The next day I went to my range and put some rounds through my rifle. There was nothing wrong with my groups.

Another evening after a lay-off of several weeks, as we were just starting out, there was, unexpectedly, a pricket against the hedge by the watercourse. I put my rifle on my sticks and engaged it, a simple shot at a sensible distance. The beast turned and sprinted back to the wood jumping the ditch like a steeplechaser. We walked over to the place and there was not a drop of blood or a hair there. Later, I found the bullet hole in the far bank of the ditch at the bottom of the hedge. I walked to the wood and the woodland floor was bare. There was no beast there! Why had I missed?

I went to the target and my first group was not even on the board. My shots were going way to the left. My rifle was "off". That explained that miss, but did not excuse me. I never should have had left it so long since last checking zero at the target.

In my low ground deerstalking career, I have seen a number of shots that have missed or wounded deer, and had the opportunity to observe and consider the reasons for them.

These fall into different categories. Deer can be missed because the deerstalker is in the wrong position: he is simply too far away. A friend of mine missed a long shot at a roe deer in the fens. He said he saw the bullet strike the earth at the deer's feet. If that's where the bullet landed the deer must have been a lot further away from the deerstalker than he allowed. Also, I suspect he, like the rest of us, had little opportunity to practice deer shooting at ranges in excess of two hundred yards distance. If it's not feasible for the stalker to practice allowing for the dropping trajectory at longer distances, it is unlikely that he is going to be routinely competent at taking occasional long shots at deer. The answer in these circumstances is to refrain from taking long shots.

Deer in woodland stalking can sometimes be encountered at very close range. The shooting of these is not as easy as one would think. A deer at ten yards would perhaps make an easy shot over open sights but nowadays everyone has a scope. Close up, high magnification can make it virtually impossible to shoot a deer at ten yards. Also, the difference in the position of the scope and the muzzle make the bullet likely to go high.

The shot typically taken off sticks at a roe buck in a high summer meadow may appear clear but will likely have some unseen stalks obstructing the target buck. The unseen, purple headed thistle stalk may readily deflect the bullet, resulting in a missed or wounded deer and leaving the stalker red faced in amazement.

There are shots before the light comes and after it has gone: there are shots snatched and shots dwelt on so long that the onlooker wonders if the rifle is taking an exam.

There are political shots. The farmer says to the stalker: "I want those deer shot. They are wrecking my crop or my trees or whatever… I want then shot!"

The stalker is immediately under pressure to shoot not just one but several. He may feel pressurised into taking a marginal shot or shots.

When the stalker (as guest or client) is out stalking under the supervision of an experienced host or professional stalker he may feel a social or a peer group pressure. The stalker host may indicate a distant beast and invite the rifle to engage it. If it is beyond the experience or capabilities of the rifle then he should decline the shot.

I was once invited to stalk on a farm on the margins of the Cheviots. Our quarry were roe bucks and we had an evening and morning outing available to us. The month was June and so each outing would be of several hours duration. My host- the shoot manager- was a roe deer stalker himself. He explained that there were roe deer on the farm (which was a large one) but that they were widely dispersed. His plan was for us to drive round, stopping for a spy at strategic observation points. He also told me that there was a buck in some new plantings that he particularly wanted shot.

We saw that buck. We saw him on the first evening. On the north side of the shoot there was a large, roughly rectangular plain, the sides of which were marked by public roads. The plain extended to several hundred acres and had on it features such as farm buildings, woods and the new plantation to which my host had referred. This plantation was situated either side of a deep, slack water dyke that went through the centre of the plain. The dyke was, according to my host, so deep as to be impossible to cross. The adjacent roads were higher than the plain and, by stopping here and there, it was possible for us to glass the plantation and the plain quite efficiently, although some parts of this were concealed. That evening, on our first attempt, we spied a group of roe deer in the middle of a field on the far side of the dyke. That " middle" was at least four hundred yards from the edge of the dyke and was unapproachable because, first, the deer on it commanded the view over the whole field and, secondly, we could not cross the dyke.

My host decided to put in a stalk along the dyke, using it's banks for cover, in the hope that the deer might move and come within range of us. They seemed restless so there was always a chance of this happening. This, in fact, is just what did happen. For some reason, perhaps a spat or just an expression of joie de vivre amongst the roe, they all ran in towards the place we had reached and, at their closest, were no more than fifty yards from us on the other side of the dyke. However, they didn't stay there and immediately ran out into the field again, before stopping two hundred or perhaps two hundred and fifty yards away. The buck stood square and presented for a shot and there was, for a few moments, a shot to be had off the sticks. I sensed my host's desire for me to shoot- in the back of my mind I knew this was a buck he needed to shoot – but held my fire. I had never engaged a paper target let alone a live deer at that distance off of sticks and had no intention of attempting that then for the very first time. The buck moved off in his own time and we carried on with our evening's stalking. My host was too polite to criticise my decision, but I understood he would have taken on that shot himself and that he must therefore have felt frustrated at the passed up opportunity.

No further beasts were seen that evening and, with it being mid summer, the time for the morning stalk came round pretty quickly. It was a memorable morning with the light arriving over the foothills of the Cheviots and I shall never forget the spies we had into all sorts of places likely to hold roe. There was the plain I have already described, a hundred acres of whin either side of a sparkling stream, deep gullies and secret valleys. We saw roe does but no bucks until late on in what would have been our last look round. On returning to the main spy place for the plain we saw the roe – the same group we had seen on the previous evening. Now, in the morning sunshine, they were much closer to the dyke bank and apparently grazing and browsing along it either in or on the edge of the plantation. Although not likely to be easy, there was a stalk to be had if we used our side of the bank of the dyke which was improved by the cover provided by the plantation.

We went away downstream to the east end of the plain and slipped into the plantation avoiding the attentions of some inquisitive, frisky steers. We stalked carefully upstream all the time using the cover of the bank, young trees and tall grasses. Eventually, we came to a mature, pollarded willow tree, one of those typical old willows with a circumference of fifteen feet or more, which by keeping it's surroundings in shade had suppressed the cover in it's vicinity. The roe deer continued to come on and were by now opposite us seventy yards away across the dyke, on the far side of the plantation. They were unhurried and I first saw the lead doe pass a gap between us, which I recognised as the only place in which I would be able to engage the buck. Two followers passed by next, taking only a few moments to cross my gap and so when the buck's head appeared I stood up and put my rifle on the fork of the sticks all in one movement. The buck took another pace or two and then paused having, I think, caught a suspicion of my movement, out of the corner of his eye. Luck favoured me as he paused with the right hand side of his chest clear and his heart exposed to the straightforward shot I now took.

The result was a fine roe buck with a nice head. The culling of him caused satisfaction to my host as the guardian of the young trees in the plantation. It confirmed for me that I had been absolutely right to pass on the shot the previous evening and to wait for an easier opportunity to cull my buck. In so doing I felt I had, for once, resisted the pressure to shoot emanating from a companion and acknowledged my own limitations. On the previous evening, the long shot may well have been within my host's routine range but it was not within mine, and an attempt would likely have resulted in an unhappy outcome with, perhaps, a wounded beast.

Sometimes, when I have taken out guests I have been aware that they have felt the same pressures that I have experienced when in their position. There is a tension that arises from the stalker and rifle relationship that makes shooting straight more difficult for the rifle than when he is alone.

On Bourn Valley Farms I have a useful observation post on what passes for a hill in Suffolk. This spot, in a dry ditch, has, as an added attraction next to it, a badger sett. On occasion I had enjoyed close up views of badgers and foxes coming and going quite unaware of me sitting quietly a few feet away. A more practical advantage is that a discreet woodland path leads from this point to the stream below. Should I see a beast coming down the slope on the other side of the stream I can nip down this path in the expectation of catching it out as it crosses the water and comes on to the grass meadow.

One early August morning I took my guest to this point and sat him down to watch and observe. We had not been there very long when a decent muntjac buck showed itself well up the watercourse. He was working his way downstream, and I knew that if I could get my guest down the path, he would likely get a safe, simple shot at the incoming buck on the bank of the watercourse. That's just what happened. I ran my guest down the woodland path and then held him up just before he reached the place where it opened out into the meadow with the stream, hidden from view by the summer herbage on it's bank on the right hand side of this. I put the sticks up and indicated to the guest that he should get ready to shoot. In such moments I admit friendship takes a back seat. If there is a shot to be had, my focus is entirely on taking it and, not just any old how, but on my terms.

Back to that morning moment, the guest got his rifle up on the fork of the sticks. I stood at his shoulder, scanning the meadow and more specifically the uncut margin. Very soon, I saw a chestnut brown shape and there was the muntjac emerging from the cover he had been investigating. He came on with that busy bustling muntjac mien that is so familiar to deerstalkers and, although the guest was twitching a little by then, I thought nothing of it as the moment was an exciting one. At fifty yards, I didn't want the buck to come any nearer and, when he obligingly turned his head to the left, I stopped him in his tracks with a low whistle. My guest shot, too quickly, and skewered the beast through it's haunches- a rank bad shot at that range. Another shot was required to finish the business and, although my client had a nice head, the carcass had two spoiled haunches and only the saddle could be salvaged.

This tale had a sequel. The following year I took the same guest back to the observation post on the hill. On this occasion we soon saw a cull roe buck, in rutting mode, surging through the wheat on the far side of the watercourse. Again, I realised that if I could get my guest to the place from which he had shot the previous year, he would have a simple chance. I signalled to him to move and got him down to the opening. I got him set up for a shot off my sticks in just the same way as I had the previous year. Then, as if to order, the buck emerged out of the cover of the stream bank and paused whilst weighing up the position. No doubt there were does and other bucks in the vicinity, but I had no need to worry about them. All my guest had to do was to shoot. And that's when it all went wrong again! At his shot the buck dropped where it stood but started kicking and wriggling and was on it's feet and gone away like the wind within a few seconds. He left on the grass a spray of blood and a few strands of hair from what I eventually concluded was a neck wound. I spent the whole day searching with my dogs and friends' dogs and did not find him that day. I shot him three days later actively rutting within a hundred yards of the same place.

It wasn't until later that I realised it was insensitive of me to take that guest back to the scene of his previous embarrassment, a firing point invested with pressure for him, and almost coercing him into another misplaced shot. I should add that my guest was generally a careful and accurate rifle shot.

Amongst my guests I have a couple of first class rifle shots. Over the course of their visits, they have shot more than their share of the cull beasts we have been hunting. Their skills have enabled them to take more, and more difficult chances, that my other guests. Their contributions have been very useful and have helped me achieve the considerable culls with which I am charged. Whichever high seat or stand I put them in, Rupert and Rory were always likely to cull a deer of some sort. This does not mean, however, that their shooting is entirely trouble free. One morning, when I picked Rupert up after an outing he confessed he had missed a muntjac. I asked if it was a clean miss and he said it was. Then I asked him why he had missed and he replied that it had been too far away. I knew the position where he had been sitting and the ride it overlooked and worked out his shot must have been taken at approaching two hundred yards range. Rupert had just learned that there is a range limit to the accuracy of a good shot such as himself, just as there is a lesser limit for a poor one. Rory's feet of clay were exposed when he was invited to shoot a roe buck off sticks during the rut. Put simply, he rapidly contracted a dose of buck fever and missed. I have no idea what caused this excellent rifle shot and experienced stalker to shake like a leaf and pull his shot like a novice. It happens!

In the deer larder, inspecting a hundred plus beasts a year, I always like to take a close look at the carcass even if I have not done the gralloch. Most of the bullet damage I see is indicative of good shooting. My stronger rifles favour the neck shot and I have seen the successful outcome of many of those. However, my strategy is to prioritise the cull and so many of the killing shots are so called engine room shots to the heart and lung area. Again, my observations time and again of the entrance and exit holes of the missile show that it must have passed through the heart or lungs.

Then there are those, and there are far fewer of them, that are a touch low or high, too far forward or back. They serve to remind me that these beasts are not shot like targets on a range at the top of the day from a purpose built firing point but at first or last light and at awkward angles under the pressure caused by the beast being alive and mobile. Having seen my best rifles make mistakes now and then I would say it's amazing there are not more of them.

Chapter Seventeen

Over My Shoulder

I T'S MANY YEARS now since that cull buck collided with my truck, and the purchase, soon afterwards, of my first deer rifle. These events were important to me as it was through them that I have discovered the most enduring and exciting passion of my sporting life.

I still manage the deer at Bourn Valley Farms, Peninsular and Maytree Farms and on the Eve Estate and on other interesting farms. Happily, I am just as excited now by a low ground stalking outing as I was in the early days, and hope that these are more productive now that I know all the different deer paths.

I am grateful to those landowners who have entrusted their deer to my management and have tried to do the best job I can for all of them in accordance with their instructions. I have enjoyed my dealings with them, and have accepted the politics of the estate and farm as part and parcel of a deer manager's lot.

Now, whilst actively out on the ground, trying to achieve today's cull I enjoy the added pleasure of recalling stalks attempted and culls achieved in previous years. Nowadays, sitting in high seats, waiting for something to happen, gives me the cue to relive past incidents, some of deer shot but more of them watched.

I never sit in my Pond High Seat without remembering the evening during which a roe doe wandered under the seat, whilst I was in it. Having passed unsuspecting ten feet below me, between the ladder of the seat and the tree it was leaning against, she disappeared into the copse immediately to my right.

There is one summer morning incident I shall never forget. Perched up in my Oak Tree High Seat before first light, my views were limited by an early morning summer mist, the sort that rolls in and out in the course of a few minutes. On that morning I could see the stubble in front of me and the standing wheat crop in the part harvested field to my left, with the mist precluding any further visibility. As I watched what ground I could see, I saw a roe doe with twin fawns step out of the standing corn. Although not long light, the doe proceeded with the greatest care and circumspection and the fawns aped her every move and pause. I was in no doubt this was lesson time with the kids acquiring survival and wariness skills from their prudent, thoughtful mother. All these years later that scene of the roe doe and her twin kids appearing out of the mist is still as fresh as it was then.

One summer morning, whilst waiting in a high seat in a wood on the Eve Estate, I watched a common coloured fallow doe and calf stroll up to a recently coppiced hazel stool, which was being protected by plastic netting supported on posts. The doe, in a laughably louche manner, leaned her full body weight on the taunt netting to enable her to reach the tasty young shoots protected by it. Her calf waited patiently whilst it's mother ate her fill and then the two of them wandered off into the thicket and were almost immediately lost from my view. I recall how relaxed the doe was , and recognised the contrast between her as a permanent summer resident in that wood and the spooky post rut herd animal she would become when she was giving me the run-around in the winter months.

Recollections of those "too- good- to-shoot" bucks observed on the same estate are particularly sweet. I never go into Cattle Grove, a wood that particularly lends itself to muntjac calling, without remembering it's late and most distinguished resident roe buck. In an area where heads are generally indifferent, the Cattle Grove Buck was king. Big in bodyweight and utterly dominant in his territory, he also had a superb six point medal head. Every rut, I would slip into Cattle Grove and call him up for inspection. An obliging buck, he would come charging in and then, suddenly becoming aware that I was no doe, would stand off for long enough for me to admire him.

152

He really was a perfect roe buck and owned that territory as of right for several seasons. What happened to him in the end is another story too long to tell here.

The big fallow bucks- all off our shooting list at Eve- were less constant in their residences. However, almost all my high seats on the heavy land side of Eve hold memories for me of big fallow bucks going about their business and I still feel a frisson of excitement when I revisit the truly magnificent, close up observations I have had of these. On all my stalking ground which hold roe deer, I have a heap of happy memories relating to roe bucks watched, called and, in some cases, shot during the rut. It is special when the stalker can walk the woods and remember a cull buck grassed here and a master buck spared there. It is sweet when a ride or a glade is invested with recollections of fox coloured bucks coming to the call.

There are so many memories I cannot record a tenth of them here. Much remains to be done; many more deer need to be culled. It's time, therefore, to end this memoir. As I write these final words, the first tinge of dawn grey colouring is seeping into the sky, so I must shoulder my rifle and head out into the fields and woods. You may catch a glimpse of me there, with the breeze in my face, forever on the deer path.